D Web Development

Leverage the power of D and the vibe.d framework to develop web applications that are incredibly fast

Kai Nacke

BIRMINGHAM - MUMBAI

D Web Development

Copyright © 2016 Packt Publishing

All rights reserved. No part of this book may be reproduced, stored in a retrieval system, or transmitted in any form or by any means, without the prior written permission of the publisher, except in the case of brief quotations embedded in critical articles or reviews.

Every effort has been made in the preparation of this book to ensure the accuracy of the information presented. However, the information contained in this book is sold without warranty, either express or implied. Neither the author, nor Packt Publishing, and its dealers and distributors will be held liable for any damages caused or alleged to be caused directly or indirectly by this book.

Packt Publishing has endeavored to provide trademark information about all of the companies and products mentioned in this book by the appropriate use of capitals. However, Packt Publishing cannot guarantee the accuracy of this information.

First published: January 2016

Production reference: 1250116

Published by Packt Publishing Ltd.
Livery Place
35 Livery Street
Birmingham B3 2PB, UK.

ISBN 978-1-78528-889-0

www.packtpub.com

Credits

Author
Kai Nacke

Reviewers
Orfeo Da Già
Stephan Dilly
Paul Féraud
Kazuki Komatsu
Adam D. Ruppe
Robert "burner" Schadek

Acquisition Editor
Tushar Gupta

Content Development Editor
Merwyn D'souza

Technical Editor
Pranil Pathare

Copy Editor
Tasneem Fatehi

Project Coordinator
Neha Bhatnagar

Proofreader
Safis Editing

Indexer
Mariammal Chettiyar

Production Coordinator
Arvindkumar Gupta

Cover Work
Arvindkumar Gupta

Foreword

As a general-purpose language, D has held good potential of being applied in the burgeoning web server domain. D's build speed makes its convenience close to that of scripting languages—the argument goes—and there's also a lot to like about the running speed of the resulting native code, too.

This has remained a theoretical possibility for a good while, until vibe.d came out of nowhere to take the D community by storm. The vibe.d framework is everything that I'd hoped it to be—a comprehensive, compelling, modern framework that wonderfully uses D's features to strike a balance between flexibility, performance, and ease of use.

It is everything I hoped... except for one thing. It doesn't have a good book teaching it properly. Therefore, it's easy to imagine my giddiness now that I was offered the honor to write this foreword for such a book.

Written by *Kai Nacke*, a long-standing and respected luminary of the D community (known among other things for LDC, the LLVM-based D compiler), *D Web Development* does an admirable job of taking its reader from not knowing much about web development (as I confess your truly is, or at least was) to getting a high-performance server up and running. Also, customizing it in so many ways: content, localization, data connectivity, interoperation, and defining extensions.

Since its creation, vibe.d has slowly but surely become one of the most important frameworks written in D and simultaneously one of the best examples of using D on large scale, so much so that vibe.d is being made part of the reference D distribution. This book is a necessary and welcome term of that equation.

Andrei Alexandrescu
Co-developer of the D programming language

About the Author

Kai Nacke is a professional IT architect living in Düsseldorf, Germany. He holds a diploma in computer science from the University of Dortmund. His diploma thesis about universal hash functions was recognized as the best of the semester. He has been with IBM for more than 15 years, and has great experience in the development and architecture of business and enterprise applications.

Fascinated by the first home computer, he learned to program a VIC-20 in BASIC. Later, he turned to Turbo PASCAL and Small C on CP/M. Experimenting with the source of Small C created his interest in compiler technology. Many computers, operating systems, and languages followed these first steps.

Around 2005, he became interested in the D programming language and created the first fun applications in D. Missing a 64-bit D compiler for Windows, he started to contribute to the LLVM compiler framework and LDC, the LLVM-based D compiler. Soon, he became committer of both projects and is now the current maintainer of LDC.

He is also a speaker at the Free and Open Source Software Developers' European Meeting (FOSDEM) and was one of the reviewers of *D Cookbook*, *Packt Publishing*.

> Writing a book is challenging. I would like to thank everybody who supported me by answering questions, accepting pull requests, or by simply encouraging me to go on. I would also like to thank the reviewers who did a great job. Their comments really contributed to the quality of the book.

About the Reviewers

Orfeo Da Vià is an Italian software developer and has been professionally developing software since 1994. Over the past four years, he has written a number of D software applications.

Orfeo is currently employed as a senior developer at Microline.

Outside the software world, Orfeo enjoys spending time with his two daughters, Raffaella and Adele, and his wife, Alessandra.

Stephan Dilly works as the head of front-end engineering at InnoGames in Germany. In the nine years of professional software development, he has worked in the games industry for Funatics and Ubisoft Blue Byte. He has also worked as a software consultant at Sopra Steria Consulting. The D programming language has been his language of choice for his spare-time projects since 2006. In 2014, Stephan was a speaker at the DConf in San Francisco, where he talked about a backend server architecture developed in D.

Paul Féraud is software engineer with passion for math, algorithms, and programming. He holds a diplôme d'Ingénieur in mechanical engineering from the École Centrale de Nantes in France and a master's degree in software engineering from Keio University in Japan.

Paul has worked for Amadeus, developing a business rule engine that is designed for very high throughput. He has also worked for Dassault Systèmes, developing the architecture backing SIMULIA's finite element simulation systems.

In parallel to this, Paul took great interest in the D programming language and began contributing to its development. He became a member of the core development team and has participated in the design and implementation of its standard library.

Paul now works for Google in Switzerland. He spends most of his time raising his beautiful daughter with his loving and supporting wife.

Kazuki Komatsu is a university student, currently majoring in wireless communication engineering. He started learning D programming language at the age of 16. He has been writing D grammar documents in Japanese and creating a variety of D libraries, such as linear algebra, compile-time meta programming, and Twitter client. Recently, Kazuki has been creating GUI toolkit, awebview, which is similar to GitHub's Electron; however, awebview is written with D and we can write GUI apps with D, HTML, CSS, and JavaScript.

Adam D. Ruppe is the author of *D Cookbook, Packt Publishing* and a long-time contributor to the D ecosystem.

Robert "burner" Schadek is a regular contributor to the standard D library, Phobos. His D journey started when he used D to create a Distributed Multithreaded Caching D compiler for his computer science master's thesis. He presented this work at DConf 2013. His commitment to Phobos can be seen all over the library. His biggest contribution to Phobos is the experimental logging framework. He is currently working on his PhD in computer science at the University of Oldenburg, Germany. There, he uses the high-performance computing (HPC) facility of the university and a lot of C++ to crunch the numbers on his original data-replication protocol. However, during his programming, he has learned one thing to be true—every untested function is buggy.

www.PacktPub.com

Support files, eBooks, discount offers, and more

For support files and downloads related to your book, please visit www.PacktPub.com.

Did you know that Packt offers eBook versions of every book published, with PDF and ePub files available? You can upgrade to the eBook version at www.PacktPub.com and as a print book customer, you are entitled to a discount on the eBook copy. Get in touch with us at service@packtpub.com for more details.

At www.PacktPub.com, you can also read a collection of free technical articles, sign up for a range of free newsletters and receive exclusive discounts and offers on Packt books and eBooks.

https://www2.packtpub.com/books/subscription/packtlib

Do you need instant solutions to your IT questions? PacktLib is Packt's online digital book library. Here, you can search, access, and read Packt's entire library of books.

Why subscribe?

- Fully searchable across every book published by Packt
- Copy and paste, print, and bookmark content
- On demand and accessible via a web browser

Free access for Packt account holders

If you have an account with Packt at www.PacktPub.com, you can use this to access PacktLib today and view 9 entirely free books. Simply use your login credentials for immediate access.

Table of Contents

Preface	**v**
Chapter 1: Getting Started with Your First Web Application	**1**
Installing the D compiler and the DUB package manager	2
Ubuntu and Debian	2
Fedora	3
OS X	4
Windows	4
Building from source	4
Verifying your environment	6
Creating your first web application	7
Using DUB to set up the project structure	7
Creating your first template	12
Summary	15
Chapter 2: Using Templates for Your Web Pages	**17**
Benefits of using templates	17
Creating your first template	19
Turning the HTML page into a Diet template	19
Adding inheritance	21
Using includes	22
Integrating other languages with blocks and filters	23
Solving common tasks	28
Configuring the document type	28
Comments in a template	29
More about tags	30
Localizing your website	31
Adding D code to your template	36
Summary	37

Table of Contents

Chapter 3: Get Interactive – Forms and Flow Control — 39
Introducing the note application — 39
Creating a template with a simple form — 40
A closer look at route matching — 46
Serving static files — 48
Storing session data — 50
Authenticating the user — 54
Using basic authentication — 55
Using digest authentication — 57
Form-based authentication — 59
Enabling TLS/SSL with your application — 62
Displaying an error page — 63
Uploading files — 65
Summary — 66

Chapter 4: Easy Forms with the Web Framework — 67
Taking advantage of unique D features — 67
Converting the note application — 69
Naming the handler functions — 69
Passing values of form fields — 70
Creating sessions and session variables — 71
Putting everything together — 71
Validating user input — 75
Displaying error messages with @errorDisplay — 75
Refining the validation — 77
Adding authentication — 80
Localizing the web content — 83
Summary — 84

Chapter 5: Accessing a Database — 85
Choosing the right database technology — 85
Relational databases — 86
A key-value store — 86
Document databases — 87
Making a choice — 88
Using the Redis key-value store — 89
Installing Redis — 89
Accessing Redis from the note application — 90
Using the MongoDB document database — 93
Installing MongoDB — 93
Persisting data with MongoDB — 94

[ii]

Table of Contents

Using the MySQL relational database	**97**
Installing MySQL	97
Using MySQL with vibe.d	97
Summary	**102**
Chapter 6: Using the REST Interface	**103**
Defining the principles of the World Wide Web	**103**
Serializing D to JSON and back	**104**
Creating and using a REST service	**106**
Providing a service	107
Using a service	109
Tailoring the generated REST API	**110**
Changing the generated path	110
Passing parameters	112
Accessing CouchDB	**113**
Installing CouchDB	113
Testing the REST interface	113
Implementing the NoteStore service	116
Summary	**120**
Chapter 7: The vibe.d Internals	**121**
The programming model of vibe.d	**121**
What is a fiber?	121
Benefits of asynchronous I/O	123
Combining threads, fibers, and asynchronous I/O	124
Coding your own main function	**125**
Performing background work	**127**
Running a fiber-based task	127
Using a thread	130
Porting an existing driver	**133**
An alternative solution for the existing drivers	**135**
Summary	**135**
Chapter 8: Using vibe.d with a GUI Client	**137**
The GUI event loop and vibe.d	**137**
Creating a Win32 GUI application	**138**
Creating an X11 GUI application	**144**
Integrating with other GUI toolkits	**149**
Summary	**149**

[iii]

Chapter 9: Power Your Application with vibe.d Extensions — 151
Publishing your project in the DUB registry — 151
Useful community projects — 153
Adding WebDAV services — 153
Running your own blog — 154
Chatting with IRC — 156
Coding for the Internet of Things — 159
Serving news — 163
Accessing the Apache Cassandra database — 164
Summary — 166
Index — 167

Preface

In the cloud age, web technologies are more important than ever. The vibe.d framework enables you to use the D programming language for a wide range of web-related tasks. The D programming language allows elegant solutions for common problems, while native compilation produces fast binaries. The vibe.d framework takes advantage of these language features. Together with the innovative use of fibers, the applications that you build are scalable and have a very quick response time.

This book will explain everything you need to know about the vibe.d framework in order to successfully build and run web applications.

What this book covers

Chapter 1, *Getting Started with Your First Web Application*, explains how to set up and use your development environment. At the end of this chapter, you will have already created your first web application.

Chapter 2, *Using Templates for Your Web Pages*, covers the Diet template engine. You will learn all about templates—from creating simple static templates to using D code in templates.

Chapter 3, *Get Interactive – Forms and Flow Control*, brings web forms to your application and introduces route matching.

Chapter 4, *Easy Forms with the Web Framework*, discusses how to validate user input.

Chapter 5, *Accessing a Database*, shows how to use a database in an application using a variety of SQL and NoSQL bases.

Preface

Chapter 6, Using the REST Interface, teaches you about REST services. You will learn how to provide and consume a generated REST service. You will also study how to interface with an existing REST service.

Chapter 7, The vibe.d Internals, introduces you to the fiber-based pseudo-blocking programming model that is the base for vibe.d.

Chapter 8, Using vibe.d with a GUI Client, applies the vibe.d programming model to a graphical UI application.

Chapter 9, Power Your Application with vibe.d Extensions, shows you what other developers have already implemented with vibe.d and how to publish your application.

What you need for this book

You need a Linux, Windows, or Mac PC that is capable of running the DMD D compiler and the DUB package manager. Both software packages are available at `http://code.dlang.org/`. The vibe.d framework requires an `SSL` library and the `libevent` library to be installed. The various sources are described in *Chapter 1, Getting Started with Your First Web Application*.

In order to compile the examples, you need an Internet connection in order to allow the automatic download of dependent software.

For the example in *Chapter 5, Accessing a Database*, you need Redis 3.x (available at `http://redis.io/`), MongoDB 3.x (available at `http://ww.mongodb.org/`), and MySQL 5.x (available at `http://dev.mysql.com/downloads/`). *Chapter 6, Using the REST Interface*, uses CouchDB (available at `http://couchdb.apache.org/`) and *Chapter 9, Power Your Application with vibe.d Extensions*, uses Cassandra (available at `http://cassandra.apache.org/`).

Who this book is for

Whether you are new to the world of D, already have developed applications in D, or you want to leverage the power of D for web development, then this book is ideal for you. Basic knowledge of core web technologies, such as HTML 5, is helpful; however, it not necessary. This book explains the complex details to speed your web development.

Conventions

In this book, you will find a number of text styles that distinguish between different kinds of information. Here are some examples of these styles and an explanation of their meaning.

Code words in text, database table names, folder names, filenames, file extensions, pathnames, dummy URLs, user input, and Twitter handles are shown as follows: "You also need to install `openssl` and `libevent`, which are used by vibe.d."

A block of code is set as follows:

```
name "hello"
description "A simple vibe.d server application."
copyright "Copyright © 2015, <yourid>"
authors "<yourid>"
dependency "vibe-d" version="~>0.7.23"
versions "VibeDefaultMain"
```

When we wish to draw your attention to a particular part of a code block, the relevant lines or items are set in bold:

```
body
  block header
    header Header
  block navigation
    include navigation
  block content
  block footer
    footer Footer
```

Any command-line input or output is written as follows:

```
$ tar xvzf dub-0.9.24.tar.gz
$ cd dub-0.9.24
$ ./build.sh
```

Preface

New terms and **important words** are shown in bold. Words that you see on the screen, for example, in menus or dialog boxes, appear in the text like this: "Click on the **Unlock** button to unlock the window and change the account type to **Administrator**."

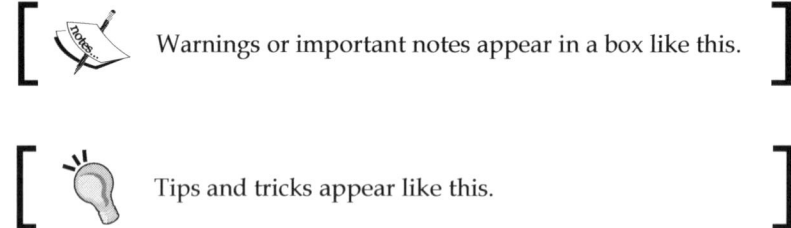

Reader feedback

Feedback from our readers is always welcome. Let us know what you think about this book—what you liked or disliked. Reader feedback is important for us as it helps us develop titles that you will really get the most out of.

To send us general feedback, simply e-mail feedback@packtpub.com, and mention the book's title in the subject of your message.

If there is a topic that you have expertise in and you are interested in either writing or contributing to a book, see our author guide at www.packtpub.com/authors.

Customer support

Now that you are the proud owner of a Packt book, we have a number of things to help you to get the most from your purchase.

Downloading the example code

You can download the example code files from your account at http://www.packtpub.com for all the Packt Publishing books you have purchased. If you purchased this book elsewhere, you can visit http://www.packtpub.com/support and register to have the files e-mailed directly to you.

Downloading the color images of this book

We also provide you with a PDF file that has color images of the screenshots/diagrams used in this book. The color images will help you better understand the changes in the output. You can download this file from https://www.packtpub.com/sites/default/files/downloads/8890OS_ColouredImages.pdf.

Errata

Although we have taken every care to ensure the accuracy of our content, mistakes do happen. If you find a mistake in one of our books—maybe a mistake in the text or the code—we would be grateful if you could report this to us. By doing so, you can save other readers from frustration and help us improve subsequent versions of this book. If you find any errata, please report them by visiting http://www.packtpub.com/submit-errata, selecting your book, clicking on the **Errata Submission Form** link, and entering the details of your errata. Once your errata are verified, your submission will be accepted and the errata will be uploaded to our website or added to any list of existing errata under the Errata section of that title.

To view the previously submitted errata, go to https://www.packtpub.com/books/content/support and enter the name of the book in the search field. The required information will appear under the **Errata** section.

Piracy

Piracy of copyrighted material on the Internet is an ongoing problem across all media. At Packt, we take the protection of our copyright and licenses very seriously. If you come across any illegal copies of our works in any form on the Internet, please provide us with the location address or website name immediately so that we can pursue a remedy.

Please contact us at copyright@packtpub.com with a link to the suspected pirated material.

We appreciate your help in protecting our authors and our ability to bring you valuable content.

Questions

If you have a problem with any aspect of this book, you can contact us at questions@packtpub.com, and we will do our best to address the problem.

Getting Started with Your First Web Application

Today's World Wide Web is shaped by sites, such as Facebook and Amazon, that handle millions of users. The **vibe.d** framework is designed to create fast and scalable web applications. A significant difference from other frameworks is the use of the **D programming language**.

In this chapter, you will learn the following:

- How to install a D compiler and the DUB package manager
- What the prerequisites of the vibe.d framework are
- What the project structure and files created by the DUB package manager are
- How to create a simple web application How to develop with the D programming language

The D programming language is a general purpose programming language that offers modern convenience, modeling power, and native efficiency with a familiar C-style syntax. If you are new to D, then you should visit `http://dlang.org/`. This site contains the language definition, references to the standard libraries, downloads for the D compiler, and a lot of other tools.

If you have any questions about D, then visit the web forum at `http://forum.dlang.org/`.

To develop an application in D, all you need is your favorite text editor and the D compiler. The vibe.d framework is used for web applications. You can find information about vibe.d and the programming documentation at `http://vibed.org/`. For any questions about vibe.d, you can use the web forum at `http://forum.rejectedsoftware.com/groups/rejectedsoftware.vibed/`.

The vibe.d framework has some external dependencies, too. It requires the event notification library **libevent** and the **OpenSSL** libraries. If you need more information about these libraries, then please visit http://libevent.org/ and https://openssl.org/.

The following section describes how to install the D compiler, package manager DUB, and dependencies on your operating system.

Installing the D compiler and the DUB package manager

The vibe.d framework is written in the D programming language. To get started, you need a D compiler and the DUB package manager. You also need to install openssl and libevent, which are used by vibe.d.

There are three major D compilers available, as follows:

- The reference compiler, **DMD** (http://dlang.org/download.html)
- The GNU compiler, **GDC** (http://gdcproject.org/downloads)
- The LLVM-based compiler, **LDC** (https://github.com/ldc-developers/ldc/releases)

You can use any of these compilers to develop with the vibe.d framework. However, the installation instructions are very different. In this book, only the DMD compiler is used.

A recommended setup is to use the DMD compiler during development and one of the other compilers to produce the final highly optimized binary.

Ubuntu and Debian

The easiest way to install DMD on Ubuntu and Debian is to use the D APT repository provided by Jordi Sayol. The website of this project is located at http://d-apt.sourceforge.net/. The steps to install DMD and DUB are as follows:

1. Open a terminal and type the following in order to add the repository sources:

    ```
    $ sudo wget http://master.dl.sourceforge.net/project/d-apt/files/d-apt.list -O /etc/apt/sources.list.d/d-apt.list
    ```

2. Then, you need to update the list of packages:

   ```
   $ sudo apt-get update
   ```

   This command complains that the public key for the d-apt repository could not be verified. The displayed fingerprint is `EBCF975E5BA24D5E`. Allow an unauthenticated install of `d-apt` and update the list of packages again:

   ```
   $ sudo apt-get -y --allow-unauthenticated install --reinstall d-apt-keyring
   $ sudo apt-get update
   ```

3. Now you are ready to install the compiler and the package manager:

   ```
   $ sudo apt-get install -y dmd-bin
   $ sudo apt-get install -y dub
   ```

4. Lastly, you need to install `openssl` and `libevent`:

   ```
   $ sudo apt-get install -y libssl-dev libevent-dev
   ```

Fedora

On Fedora, you use the pre-built compiler binary from the `dlang.org` website. There is no package for the DUB package manager therefore, you must built this tool from the source. Refer to http://dlang.org/download.html and download the Fedora package of the DMD compiler. The available version at the time of writing this book is 2.068.2. You may need to change the version number when a new version of the compiler is released. The instructions are given for Fedora 22 or later. If you use Fedora 21 or earlier, then replace the `dnf` command with `yum`. The steps to install the DMD complier are as follows:

1. To install `dmd`, type in a terminal:

   ```
   $ sudo dnf install -y dmd-2.068.2-0.fedora.x86_64.rpm
   ```

2. Install the required `openssl` and `libevent` libraries. You also need to install the development package of `libcurl` that is used to compile `dub`:

   ```
   $ sudo dnf install -y openssl-devel libevent-devel libcurl-devel
   ```

3. After that, go to http://code.dlang.org/download and download **source tarball** of DUB. The current version number is 0.9.24. Again, you need to change the version number if a newer version is available. To compile and install, just type the following:

   ```
   $ tar xvzf dub-0.9.24.tar.gz
   $ cd dub-0.9.24
   $ ./build.sh
   $ sudo cp bin/dub /usr/local/bin
   ```

Getting Started with Your First Web Application

>  If you get an error message that you are not in the list of sudoers, then you need to change the type of your user to administrator. Open system settings and click on **Users**. Click on the **Unlock** button to unlock the window and change the account type to **Administrator**. Now you can use the sudo command.

OS X

To install the D compiler and the DUB package manager, you can use the **Homebrew** package manager (http://brew.sh/):

1. Open a terminal and first update the formulae:

   ```
   $ brew update
   ```

2. Now install the D compiler:

   ```
   $ brew install dmd
   ```

3. Next, you will install the DUB package manger:

   ```
   $ brew install dub
   ```

4. Lastly, you need to install openssl and libevent:

   ```
   $ brew install openssl libevent
   ```

Windows

On Windows, you will simply use the pre-built binaries from the dlang.org website. Go to http://dlang.org/download.html and download the Windows EXE file of the DMD compiler. Double-click on the downloaded file in order to start the installer and then follow the instructions on the screen. The D compiler is now ready to use.

DUB is installed in a similar way. Go to http://code.dlang.org/download and download the installer for Windows. Double-click on the downloaded file to start the installer and then follow the instructions on the screen as done previously.

Building from source

You can also build the applications from source. For some systems, (for example, FreeBSD, Solaris x86, and Linux on non-Intel platforms) this is the only way to install the software. The following are the instructions for a **Portable Operating System Interface (POSIX)** for a Unix system.

At the time when this book was written, the compiler itself was translated from C++ to D. Version 2.068 is the first one that requires a D compiler for bootstrap. Therefore, you need to install version 2.067.1 before you can install the current version of the compiler.

At build time, you need the GNU C/C++ compiler (gcc/g++) and GNU make (gmake). Using another compiler or make tool may work but is not well tested. For Phobos (the D standard library), you need to have `libcurl` installed. If your distribution does not provide `libcurl`, then you can find the source and install the instructions at the `http://curl.haxx.se/libcurl/` website.

The easiest way to build DMD from source is using the GitHub repository. First, you build version 2.067.1. This creates a D compiler that you will then use to compile the final version that you want to install, as follows:

1. Change to your working directory. Then, check the sources from GitHub:

    ```
    $ for i in dmd druntime phobos; do
        git clone https://github.com/D-Programming-Language/$i.git;
      done
    ```

2. Now, check out version 2.067.1, as follows:

    ```
    $ for i in dmd druntime phobos; do
        (cd $i && git checkout v2.067.1);
      done
    ```

3. Compile the D compiler and install it to `/tmp/dmd` as shown in the following code. The CPU model (32 bit or 64 bit) is automatically determined by the makefile. If this fails, you can add `MODEL=32` (for 32 bit) or `MODEL=64` (for 64 bit) to the `make` command:

    ```
    $ for i in dmd druntime phobos; do
        make -C $i -f posix.mak install INSTALL_DIR=/tmp/dmd
      done
    ```

4. Now clean the directories:

    ```
    $ for i in dmd druntime phobos; do
        make -C $i -f posix.mak clean
      done
    ```

5. Next, check out the version of the compiler that you prefer using. Currently, it is 2.068.2:

    ```
    $ for i in dmd druntime phobos; do
        git checkout v2.068.2
      done
    ```

Getting Started with Your First Web Application

6. Then, you can compile and install the version of the compiler. You need to specify the previously installed compiler. The binary is found in sub-folders specifying the operating system and CPU model, for example, `linux/bin64` or `freebsd/bin32`:

   ```
   $ make -C dmd -f posix.mak HOST_DC=/tmp/dmd/linux/bin64/dmd
     install INSTALL_DIR=~/dmdss
   $ make -C druntime -f posix.mak install INSTALL_DIR=~/dmd
   $ make -C phobos -f posix.mak install INSTALL_DIR=~/dmd
   ```

7. The last step is to add the compiler to your `PATH` environment variable. The syntax depends on the shell you use. For bash, you run:

   ```
   $ export PATH=~/dmd:$PATH
   ```

 Building the DMD compiler on Windows differs from these generic instructions as you need the Digital Mars C/C++ compiler. I recommend using the binary download for Windows. You can find detailed build instructions for all supported systems in the wiki at http://wiki.dlang.org/Building_DMD.

The DUB package manager is written in D. Go to http://code.dlang.org/download and download the source code archive. Under the file, change the current directory of your shell to the `dub-0.9.24` folder and build the application with the following commands. You may need to replace the current version number 0.9.24 with the version you downloaded.

```
$ tar xvzf dub-0.9.24.tar.gz
$ cd dub-0.9.24
$ ./build.sh
```

You'll find the binary in the `bin` folder. You can add this folder to your `PATH` variable or copy the file to a standard folder, for example, `/usr/local/bin`:

```
$ cp bin/dub /usr/local/bin
```

Verifying your environment

Before you start coding, it is a good idea to check whether the tools work as expected. Run the following command:

```
$ dmd
```

You should see the help text provided by the compiler. The version number should be the same as the version you have downloaded.

On Linux and other POSIX systems, you can also check whether the additional libraries are installed. Run the following command:

```
$ touch empty.d && dmd -main empty.d -L-lssl -L-levent && ./empty
```

It should produce no error messages.

An error, most likely, indicates that the **libevent** library or the **OpenSSL** library is not installed on your system. You should check the install instructions that are mentioned previously for common systems. If your system is not mentioned, then you should consult the manual of your OS to know how to install additional software. If your OS does not provide these libraries, then you have to install them from source. You can find install instructions and the source archive for libevent at http://libevent.org/. The https://openssl.org/ OpenSSL site provides install instructions and the source archive. You can check your DUB installation simply by running the following command:

```
$ dub help
```

This prints the help text from DUB. The version number should be the same as the version that you have downloaded.

Creating your first web application

After you have set up your development environment, you are ready to create your first web application.

Using DUB to set up the project structure

The DUB package manager is used to package and build D applications and libraries. The tool can also be used to create the recommended project structure. You need to provide a folder name for your project and an optional project type. The project type can be `minimal`, `vibe.d`, or `deimos`. The project type determines which folders and files are created by running `dub`. The `minimal` project type creates the folders and files for a console application while `vibe.d` creates a vibe.d server application. The `deimos` project type is used for bindings to C libraries. (Refer to https://github.com/D-Programming-Deimos for the already available bindings.) If no project type is given, the package manager assumes `minimal` as the project type.

In a terminal, change your current directory to a folder where your projects should live. Run the following command:

```
$ dub init hello --type=vibe.d
Successfully created an empty project in '/<your path>/hello'.
```

This creates a new folder named `hello`. Let's look into the folder:

- A file named `dub.sdl` was created
- The `public`, `source`, and `views` folders were created
- The `source` folder contains a file named `app.d`

The `dub.sdl` file is the package description and the `app.d` file is a sample vibe.d application. The `public` and `views` folders are for public and UI related files. Open the `dub.sdl` file in your editor:

```
name "hello"
description "A simple vibe.d server application."
copyright "Copyright © 2015, <yourid>"
authors "<yourid>"
dependency "vibe-d" version="~>0.7.23"
versions "VibeDefaultMain"
```

The file uses a description in **Simple Declarative Language (SDLang)**. SDLang was designed for describing data structures and data types. It is well suited for configuration files and build specification. You can find the language specification at https://sdlang.org/.

In its simplest form, a declaration consists of a name and a value or an attribute. In the preceding `dub.sdl` file, `dependency` is a name, `"vibe-d"` is a value, and the key/value pair `version="~>0.7.23"` is an attribute. To create a nested data structure, you use { and } to specify the inner data.

It is also possible to specify more than one value or attribute. This creates a list or mapping table.

A name must start with a Unicode letter or an underscore. It can be then followed by zero or more Unicode letters, numbers, underscores, dashes, periods, and dollar signs. The format of the value depends on the data type. The most basic specifications are strings, integer numbers, and booleans: `"vibe-d"` and `` `vibe-d` `` are strings. `123` is a signed 32 bit number and `123L` a signed 64 bit number. The possible Boolean values are `true` and `false` or `on` and `off`. The language specification defines some more data types such as date values. If you need to use these data types, please use the language specification available at the previously mentioned link to look up the exact format.

Prior to DUB version 0.9.24, the package description was specified in a file called dub.json in the JSON format. While JSON support stays available (and is used by many available packages), this book uses the new SDLang format.

The fields in the dub.sdl file have the following meaning:

Name	Description
name	The name of the package. It is used to uniquely identify the package. It must only consist of lower case ASCII alpha-numeric characters, '-', and '_'. This field is required.
description	A brief description of the package.
copyright	The copyright declaration.
authors	The authors of the package.
dependency	A single dependency. The value specifies the name. Attributes version and path are used to specify the required version and a location in the file system.
versions	A list of version identifiers that to be defined during compilation.

There are many more fields available. You can find a complete list at http://code.dlang.org/package-format?lang=sdl.

Our goal is to create a web application with the vibe.d framework. DUB has automatically created a dependency to vibe.d in the package description for us.

Dependencies are specified as `"name" version="version-string"`. The name is the name of the package that we are depending on. This explains why the name must be unique; without a unique name, the package manager would not be able to resolve the dependency.

The version string consists of an operator and the version number. This allows you to restrict the version of the required packages. The possible values are as follows:

- Restrict to a certain minor version: `"~>2.2.13"`, equivalent to `">=2.2.13 <2.3.0"`
- Restrict to a certain major version: `"~>2.2"`, equivalent to `">=2.2.0 <3.0.0"`
- Require a certain version: `"==1.3.0"`
- Require a minimum version: `">=1.3.0"`
- Require a version range: `">=1.3.0 <=1.3.4"`

Getting Started with Your First Web Application

The recommended way is to use the "~>" operator. This allows flexible updates and should prevent unexpected code breakages. DUB looks up the available versions of a package in the DUB package registry at http://code.dlang.org/. The developers define the version number in their repository, for example, in GitHub. You can find more information about providing your own DUB packages in *Chapter 9, Power your Application with vibe.d Extensions*.

Our first application is quite simple. The application uses the main() function provided by vibe.d. This requires passing the VibeDefaultMain version identifier to the compiler. Compiler and linker switches are specified using build settings. The main() function is automatically provided if this version identifier is specified.

The use of compiler and linker switches depends on the operating system, processor architecture, and used compiler. DUB supports this with the platform attribute. The platform attribute contains the predefined platform identifiers that are converted to lower case and separated by dashes. The order of the identifiers is os-architecture-compiler. You can find the complete list in the D language reference at http://dlang.org/version.html#PredefinedVersions. Each part is optional. For example, platform="windows-x86_64-ldc" or platform="dmd".

DUB has created a small application, too. The source of the app.d module is as follows:

```
import vibe.d;

shared static this()
{
  auto settings = new HTTPServerSettings;
  settings.port = 8080;
  settings.bindAddresses = ["::1", "127.0.0.1"];
  listenHTTP(settings, &hello);

  logInfo("Please open http://127.0.0.1:8080/ in your browser.");
}

void hello(HTTPServerRequest req, HTTPServerResponse res)
{
  res.writeBody("Hello, World!");
}
```

The functionality is quite simple. As the `main()` function is provided by the framework, a `shared static this()` module constructor is used. This constructor is run at application startup before the `main()` function is run. In the constructor, a new `HTTPServerSettings` object is created. In the following two lines, the port number is set to `8080` and the IP address that the server listens to is set to localhost (IPv4: `127.0.0.1`, IPv6: `::1`). After that, the HTTP server is started with a call to `listenHTTP()`. Each request is handled by the `hello()` function, which only writes the string `"Hello, world!"` as the response.

You simply run `dub` in the `hello` folder in order to compile and run the application. DUB automatically resolves, downloads, and compiles all specified dependencies. Some of the downloaded libraries are only D bindings to the already installed libraries. For example, DUB downloads the D bindings for the OpenSSL library, which must be installed separately. If you run DUB for the first time, the tool fetches all dependencies which looks like this:

```
$ dub
Fetching memutils 0.4.1 (getting selected version)...
Placing memutils 0.4.1 to /home/<yourid>/.dub/packages/...
Fetching vibe-d 0.7.25 (getting selected version)...
Placing vibe-d 0.7.25 to /home/<yourid>/.dub/packages/...
Fetching libevent 2.0.1+2.0.16 (getting selected version)...
Placing libevent 2.0.1+2.0.16 to /home/<yourid>/.dub/packages/...
Fetching openssl 1.1.4+1.0.1g (getting selected version)...
Placing openssl 1.1.4+1.0.1g to /home/<yourid>/.dub/packages/...
Fetching libev 5.0.0+4.04 (getting selected version)...
Placing libev 5.0.0+4.04 to /home/<yourid>/.dub/packages/...
Fetching libasync 0.7.5 (getting selected version)...
Placing libasync 0.7.5 to /home/<yourid>/.dub/packages/...
Performing "debug" build using dmd for x86_64.
vibe-d 0.7.25: building configuration "libevent"...
hello ~master: building configuration "application"...
Linking...
Running ./hello
Listening for HTTP requests on ::1:8080
Listening for HTTP requests on 127.0.0.1:8080
Please open http://127.0.0.1:8080/ in your browser.
```

Getting Started with Your First Web Application

Open your browser and type `http://127.0.0.1:8080/` as address. You see a nice greeting from your first vibe.d application:

> **Downloading the example code**
>
> You can download the example code files from your account at `http://www.packtpub.com` for all the Packt Publishing books you have purchased. If you purchased this book elsewhere, you can visit `http://www.packtpub.com/support` and register to have the files e-mailed directly to you.

Creating your first template

The sample application that is generated by DUB returns only a text string to the browser. Of course, a real web application returns HTML 5 nowadays!

The vibe.d framework includes a template engine, the so-called **Diet** templates. Templates are used to construct an HTML page from various reusable pieces, for example, a header and navigation bar. They also enable you to place values that are calculated in your application in the generated HTML page. You can learn about the details of templates in *Chapter 2, Using Templates for Your Web Pages*. For the first application, you create a template for a simple HTML 5 page.

Run `dub` again to create a new project:

```
$ dub init hello2 --type=vibe.d
Successfully created an empty project in '/<your path>/hello2'.
```

You can put UI related files, such as HTML pages and templates, in the `views` folder. Create an `index.dt` file in the `views` folder:

```
doctype html
html
  head
    title Greetings from vibe.d
  body
    p Hello, World!
```

The template syntax resembles the HTML syntax and should be understandable if you know HTML. This is a so-called static template since there are no dynamic parts involved, for example, printing the value of a variable.

Next, you need to change the generated `source/app.d` application to contain the following source:

```
import vibe.d;

shared static this()
{
  auto settings = new HTTPServerSettings;
  settings.port = 8080;
  settings.bindAddresses = ["::1", "127.0.0.1"];
  listenHTTP(settings, staticTemplate!"index.dt");

  logInfo("Please open http://127.0.0.1:8080/ in your browser.");
}
```

In the `listenHTTP()` call, replace `&hello` with `staticTemplate!"index.dt"`. After that, delete the `hello()` function. This is all you need to do in order to use a static template!

Run `dub` to compile and run the application:

```
$ dub
Compiling diet template 'index.dt'...
 x86_64.
vibe-d 0.7.25: target for configuration "libevent" is up to date.
hello2 ~master: building configuration "application"...
Linking...
To force a rebuild of up-to-date targets, run again with --force.
Running ./hello2
Listening for HTTP requests on ::1:8080
Listening for HTTP requests on 127.0.0.1:8080
Please open http://127.0.0.1:8080/ in your browser.
```

Getting Started with Your First Web Application

Open your browser and type `http://127.0.0.1:8080/` in the address bar. You will see a similar greeting as that from your first vibe.d application. Please note that now there is a title displayed. You should also check whether the browser has received an HTML page—simply inspect the page source using facility from your favorite browser.

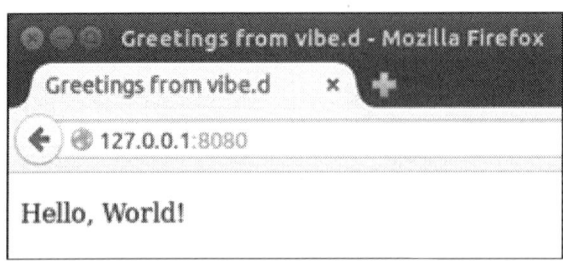

You may have noticed that this run of DUB was a bit faster and the output was different. The main functionality offered by DUB is the automatic resolution of dependencies. Our application lists vibe.d as a dependency. On the first run, DUB automatically downloads vibe.d. In order to find the package, DUB uses the public registry at `http://code.dlang.org/`. (There are many useful packages available. You will learn about the most important ones in *Chapter 9, Power your Application with vibe.d Extensions*. For now, just scroll through the list to get an impression of what is already available.)

The vibe.d framework itself has dependencies. DUB downloads them until all dependencies are resolved. After this step, the libraries and your application are compiled.

On every subsequent invocation of DUB, the dependencies are already resolved and the libraries are only linked with, and no longer have to be compiled. The second invocation is, therefore, faster and produces less output.

You can find the downloaded packages in your home directory in the `${HOME}/.dub/packages` hidden folder on Linux or `%HOMEDRIVE%%HOMEPATH%\AppData\Roaming\dub` on Windows. If you delete the folder or one of the packages inside, then DUB will re-download and recompile the missing packages on the next invocation. Most importantly, you will find the vibe.d package including its source code in this folder!

DUB provides some useful options. You can see them if you pass the `--help` flag after the `run` command (the default command that is invoked if no command is given):

```
$ dub run --help
```

Two options are very useful: `--force` and `--verbose`. With `--force`, you can force a recompilation even if nothing has changed. The `--verbose` option prints diagnostic output. This can be helpful if you need to track down an error.

Summary

In this chapter, you learned how to set up your development environment and create your first D web application. You installed the DMD compiler, DUB package manager, and some required libraries. Then, you used these tools to generate a simple web application. You changed the application to use a template in order to create HTML instead of simple text.

Equipped with this knowledge, you are now ready to dive deeper into the template engine that is explained in the next chapter.

2
Using Templates for Your Web Pages

Every website has some recurring elements, for example, a navigation bar and a header. A template engine enables you to put these elements in separate files and construct the whole page out of these files. The vibe.d includes a template engine, the so-called Diet templates.

In this chapter, you will learn the following:

- Why templates are useful
- Key concepts of Diet templates: inheritance, includes, and blocks
- How to use filters and how to create your own filter
- How to change the document type
- How to insert comments in a template
- How to localize a template
- Using D code in the templates

Benefits of using templates

Let's look at a simple HTML 5 page with a header, footer, navigation bar, and some content:

```
<!DOCTYPE html>
<html>
  <head>
    <meta charset="utf-8">
    <title>Demo site</title>
    <link rel="stylesheet" type="text/css" href="demo.css" />
```

Using Templates for Your Web Pages

```html
    </head>
    <body>
      <header>
        Header
      </header>
      <nav>
        <ul>
          <li><a href="link1">Link 1</a></li>
          <li><a href="link2">Link 2</a></li>
          <li><a href="link3">Link 3</a></li>
        </ul>
      </nav>
      <article>
        <h1>Title</h1>
        <p>Some content here.</p>
      </article>
      <footer>
        Footer
      </footer>
    </body>
</html>
```

The formatting is done with the `demo.css` file:

```css
body {
  font-size: 1em;
  color: black;
  background-color: white;
  font-family: Arial;
}
header {
  display: block;
  font-size: 200%;
  font-weight: bolder;
  text-align: center;
}
footer {
  clear: both;
  display: block;
  text-align: center;
}
nav {
  display: block;
  float: left;
  width: 25%;
```

```
    }
    article {
      display: block;
      float: left;
    }
```

Despite being simple, this page has elements that you will often find on other websites. If you create a website with more than one page, then you will be using this structure on every page in order to provide a consistent user interface. Starting with the second page, you would violate the **Don't Repeat Yourself** (**DRY**) principle: The header and footer are the elements with fixed content. The content of the navigation bar is also fixed but not every item is always displayed. Only the real content of the page (in the `article` block) changes with every page.

Templates solve this problem. A common approach while using templates is to define a base template with the page structure. For each page, you will define a template that inherits from the base template and adds the real content.

Creating your first template

In the following example, you will create a Diet template from the HTML page using various techniques. The template syntax is concise and easy to read, which is a great advantage over using plain HTML.

Turning the HTML page into a Diet template

Let's start with a one-to-one translation of the HTML page into a Diet template. The syntax that we will use is based on Jade templates (http://jade-lang.com/), which you might already be familiar with. It looks similar to the following:

```
doctype html
html
  head
    meta(charset='utf-8')
    title Demo site
    link(rel='stylesheet', type='text/css', href='demo.css')
  body
    header
      | Header
    nav
      ul
        li
          a(href='link1') Link 1
        li
```

Using Templates for Your Web Pages

```
          a(href='link2') Link 2
        li
          a(href='link3') Link 3
    article
      h1 Title
      p Some content here.
    footer
      | Footer
```

The template resembles the HTML page. Here are the basic syntax rules for a template:

- The first word on a line is an HTML tag
- The attributes of an HTML tag are written as a comma-separated list surrounded by parentheses
- A tag may be followed by plain text that may contain the HTML code
- Any plain text on a new line starts with the pipe symbol
- Nesting of elements is done by adding indentation

If you want to see the result of this template, save the code as `index.dt` and put it together with the `demo.css` file in the `views` folder of the template application from *Chapter 1, Getting Started with Your First Web Application.*

Now, you need to create a small application to see the result of the template, as shown in the following:

1. Create a new `template` project with dub:

   ```
   $ dub init template --type=vibe.d
   ```

2. Save the template as the `views/index.dt` file.
3. Copy the `demo.css` file in the `public` folder.
4. Change the contents of the generated `source/app.d` application to the following:

   ```
   import vibe.d;

   shared static this()
   {
       auto router = new URLRouter;
       router.get("/", staticTemplate!"index.dt");
       router.get("*", serveStaticFiles("public/"));

       auto settings = new HTTPServerSettings;
       settings.port = 8080;
   ```

```
        settings.bindAddresses = ["::1", "127.0.0.1"];
        listenHTTP(settings, router);

        logInfo("Please open http://127.0.0.1:8080/ in your
          browser.");
    }
```

5. Run `dub` in the project folder to start the application and then go to `http://127.0.0.1:8080/` to see the resulting page.

The application uses a new `URLRouter` class. This class is used to map a URL to a web page. With the `router.get("/", staticTemplate!"index.dt");` statement, every request for the base URL is responded by rendering of the `index.dt` template. The `router.get("*", serveStaticFiles("public/"));` statement uses a wildcard to serve all other requests as static files stored in the `public` folder.

Adding inheritance

Up to now, the template was only a one-to-one translation of the HTML page. The next step is to split the `index.dt` file from the previous section in two, `layout.dt` and `index.dt`. The `layout.dt` file will define the general structure of a page while `index.dt` inherits from this file and adds new content.

The key to using the template inheritance is in the definition of a block. A block has a name and contains some template code. A child template may replace the block, append or prepend content to a block. In the following `layout.dt` file, there are four blocks defined: `header`, `navigation`, `content`, and `footer`. For all the blocks except the `content`, a default text entry is defined, as shown in the following:

```
doctype html
html
    head
        meta(charset='utf-8')
        title Demo site
        link(rel='stylesheet', type='text/css', href='demo.css')
    body
        block header
            header Header
        block navigation
            nav
                ul
                    li <a href="link1">Link 1</a>
                    li <a href="link2">Link 2</a>
                    li <a href="link3">Link 3</a>
        block content
        block footer
            footer Footer
```

The template in the `index.dt` file inherits this layout and replaces the `content` block, as follows:

```
extends layout
block content
    article
        h1 Title
        p Some content here.
```

You can put both the files in the `views` folder and run `dub` again. The rendered page in your browser will still look the same as before.

You can now add more pages and reuse the layout. It is also possible to change the common elements that you have defined in the `header`, `footer`, and `navigation` blocks.

There is no restriction on the level of inheritance used. This allows you to construct very sophisticated template systems.

Using includes

Inheritance is not the only way to avoid repetition of template code. With the `include` keyword, you can insert the contents of another file. This allows you to place the reusable template code in separate files. As an example, just put the navigation in a separate `navigation.dt` file, as follows:

```
nav
    ul
        li <a href="link1">Link 1</a>
        li <a href="link2">Link 2</a>
        li <a href="link3">Link 3</a>
```

The `layout.dt` file uses the `include` keyword to insert the `navigation.dt` file, as shown in the following code:

```
doctype html
html
  head
    meta(charset='utf-8')
    title Demo site
    link(rel='stylesheet', type='text/css', href='demo.css')
  body
    block header
      header Header
    block navigation
```

[22]

```
        include navigation
    block content
    block footer
        footer Footer
```

Just as with the inheritance example, you can put both the files in the `views` folder and run `dub` again. The rendered page in your browser will look the same as before.

Integrating other languages with blocks and filters

So far, the templates only used the HTML content. However, a web application is usually built with a combination of languages that are often integrated in a single document, as shown in the following:

- CSS styles are placed in the `style` element
- The JavaScript code is kept in the the `script` element
- The content is typically written in a simplified markup language, such as **Markdown**

Diet templates have two mechanisms that can be used for integration of other languages.

If a tag is followed by a dot, then the block is treated as plain text. For example, look at the following template code:

```
p.
    Some text
    And some more text
```

This is translated into:

```
<p>
    Some text
    And some more text
</p>
```

The same can be used for scripts and styles, too. For example, look at the following `script` tag with JavaScript code in it:

```
script(type='text/javascript').
    console.log('D is awesome')
```

It translates into the following code:

```
<script type="text/javascript">
    console.log('D is awesome')
</script>
```

An alternative is to use a filter. You can specify a filter with a colon that is followed by the filter name. The script example can be written with a filter as follows:

```
:javascript
    console.log('D is awesome')
```

This is translated into the following:

```
<script type="text/javascript">
    //<![CDATA[
    console.log('D is awesome')
    //]]>
</script>
```

The following filters are provided by vibe.d:

- The `javascript` filter for the JavaScript code
- The `css` filter for CSS styles
- The `markdown` filter for the content that is written in the Markdown syntax
- The `htmlescape` filter to escape HTML symbols

The `css` filter works in the same way as the `javascript` filter.

The `markdown` filter accepts the text written in the Markdown syntax and translates it into HTML. Markdown is a simplified markup language for web authors, among other things. The syntax is available on the web at http://daringfireball.net/projects/markdown/syntax. The following is our previous template; however, using the `markdown` filter for the navigation and article content this time. The `navigation.dt` file now contains the following code:

```
nav
  ul
    :markdown
      - [Link 1](link1)
      - [Link 2](link2)
      - [Link 3](link3)
```

The content of the `index.dt` file will look as shown in the following:

```
extends layout
block content
  article
    :markdown
      Title
      =====

      Some content here.
```

The rendered HTML page remains the same. The advantage is that you have significantly less to type, which is beneficial if you produce a lot of content. The syntax is also easy to read, which helps in order to concentrate on the topic.

A normal plain text block can contain HTML tags, as follows:

```
p.
    Click this <a href="link">link</a>
```

This is rendered as the following:

```
<p>
    Click this <a href="link">link</a>
</p>
```

There are situations where you may want to treat HTML tags as plain text, for example, if you want to explain the HTML syntax to the reader. In this case, you can use the `htmlescape` filter:

```
p
    :htmlescape
        Link syntax: <a href="url target">text to display</a>
```

This will be rendered as the following:

```
<p>
    Link syntax: &lt;a href="url target"&gt;text to
        display&lt;/a&gt;
</p>
```

Using Templates for Your Web Pages

You can also add your own filters; vibe.d provides the `registerDietTextFilter()` function to register new filters. This function takes the name of the filter and a pointer to the filter function. The filter function itself is called with the text to filter and level of indentation, and returns the filtered text. The level of indentation tells you by how many tabs a HTML tag would be indented at this line of the output. This is important if you want to output a visually correct indentation. For example, you can use this functionality for pretty printing of D code, as follows:

1. First, create a new project with `dub`, as shown here:

   ```
   $ dub init filter --type=vibe.d
   ```

2. Then, create an `index.dt` template file in the `views` folder. Implement a new filter called `dcode` to format the D code:

   ```
   doctype html
   head
     title Code filter example
     :css
       .keyword { color: #0000ff;
           font-weight: bold; }
   body
     p You can create your own functions.
     :dcode
       T max(T)(T a, T b) {
         if (a > b) return a;
         return b;
       }
   ```

3. Place the filter function in the `app.d` file in the `source` folder. The filter function outputs the text in a `<pre>` tag. Identifier keywords are inserted in the `<span class="keyword">` element in order to allow custom formatting. For simplicity, this implementation only matches the `if` and `return` D keywords. If you want to complete the filter, then you can use the D keyword list provided at `http://dlang.org/lex.html#Keyword`. The whole application is then as shown in the following code:

   ```
   import vibe.d;

   string filterDCode(string text, size_t indent)
   {
       import std.regex;
       import std.array;

       auto dst = appender!string;
       filterHTMLEscape(dst, text,
   ```

```
                    HTMLEscapeFlags.escapeQuotes);
    auto regex = regex(r"(^|\s)(if|return)(;|\s)");
    text = replaceAll(dst.data, regex,
                `$1<span class="keyword">$2</span>$3`);

    auto indent_string = "\n" ~ "\t".replicate(indent);

    auto ret = appender!string();
    ret ~= indent_string ~ "<pre>\n"
        ~ text
        ~ indent_string ~ "</pre>";

    return ret.data;
}

shared static this()
{
    registerDietTextFilter("dcode", &filterDCode);

    auto settings = new HTTPServerSettings;
    settings.port = 8080;
    settings.bindAddresses = ["::1", "127.0.0.1"];
    listenHTTP(settings, staticTemplate!"index.dt");

    logInfo("Please open http://127.0.0.1:8080/ in your browser.");
}
```

The `filterDCode()` function uses scoped imports. Functions and types from the `std.regex` and `std.array` modules are imported in the function. This limits the scope of the imported symbols; however, it also emphasizes that the function is using these symbols.

The overall structure of the `filterDCode()` function is simple. First, the whole input text in the `text` parameter is escaped using an HTML filter. This replaces all characters with a special meaning in HTML with HTML entities. Then the `<span>` elements are inserted with the help of a regular expression and a global replace. Next, the indentation string for the `<pre>` tag is created using the `replicate()` function. The last step is to append all the strings together and return the result.

Compile and run this application to see that the keywords are shown in bold and colorized blue.

Solving common tasks

Having mastered the template basics, you will soon need to solve some common tasks. You will learn about the most common ones in the following sections.

Configuring the document type

The document type at the beginning of a page tells the browser how to render the page. All the previous examples used the `doctype` shortcut of HTML 5: `<!DOCTYPE html>`. If you need a different document type, then you have to choose between either using the built-in `doctypes` or custom `doctypes`. The following shortcuts are available:

Shortcut	Generated DOCTYPE
`doctype html`	`<!DOCTYPE html>`
`doctype xml`	`<?xml version="1.0" encoding="utf-8" ?>`
`doctype transitional`	`<!DOCTYPE html PUBLIC "-//W3C//DTD XHTML 1.0 Transitional//EN" "http://www.w3.org/TR/xhtml1/DTD/xhtml1-transitional.dtd">`
`doctype strict`	`<!DOCTYPE html PUBLIC "-//W3C//DTD XHTML 1.0 Strict//EN" "http://www.w3.org/TR/xhtml1/DTD/xhtml1-strict.dtd">`
`doctype frameset`	`<!DOCTYPE html PUBLIC "-//W3C//DTD XHTML 1.0 Frameset//EN" "http://www.w3.org/TR/xhtml1/DTD/xhtml1-frameset.dtd">`
`doctype 1.1`	`<!DOCTYPE html PUBLIC "-//W3C//DTD XHTML 1.1//EN" "http://www.w3.org/TR/xhtml11/DTD/xhtml11.dtd">`
`doctype basic`	`<!DOCTYPE html PUBLIC "-//W3C//DTD XHTML Basic 1.1//EN" "http://www.w3.org/TR/xhtml-basic/xhtml-basic11.dtd">`
`doctype mobile`	`<!DOCTYPE html PUBLIC "-//WAPFORUM//DTD XHTML Mobile 1.2//EN" "http://www.openmobilealliance.org/tech/DTD/xhtml-mobile12.dtd">`

If you need another document type, you can write the specification after the `doctype` tag. For example, you can generate the HTML 4 Transitional `doctype` with the following code:

```
doctype html PUBLIC "-//W3C//DTD HTML 4.01 Transitional//EN"
  "http://www.w3.org/TR/html4/loose.dtd"
```

In general, it is recommended to use HTML 5 for new web applications.

Comments in a template

Like any other piece of code, you may want to add comments to your templates. Diet templates support the single line // D style comment. Such a comment is rendered as an HTML comment, for example:

```
// This is a comment.
```

It is rendered as the following:

```
<!-- This is a comment -->
```

If you don't want the comment to show up in the rendered HTML, then you may use //- instead:

```
//- Not visible in HTML
```

You can even use a comment block:

```
body
    //
        Comment line 1
        Comment line 2
```

The preceding code is rendered as follows:

```
<body>
    <!--
        Comment line 1
        Comment line 2
    -->
</body>
```

As done previously, use //- if you don't want the comment to show up in the rendered HTML page.

An important use case for comments is the conditional comment for use with the Internet Explorer browser. This is supported with a general mechanism. If a line starts with the < character, then the whole line is treated as plain text. For example, take a look at the following code:

```
<!--[if IE]>
p Shown only by Internet Explorer (up to version 10)
<![endif]-->
<!--[if !IE]> -->
p Shown by all other browsers
<!-- <![endif]-->
```

It is rendered as the following:

```
<!--[if IE]>
<p>Shown only by Internet Explorer (up to version 10)</p>
<![endif]-->
<!--[if !IE]> -->
<p>Shown by all other browsers</p>
<!-- <![endif]-->
```

Please note the use of the standard HTML comment in the `if !IE` branch. This is necessary as other browsers may not interpret the conditional comment.

> Conditional comments are no longer supported in standard and quirks modes since Internet Explorer 10.

You can use this syntax to insert any tag in the rendered document. However, blocks are not supported, which restricts the usefulness of the feature to a single line.

More about tags

You have already learned how to add attributes to a tag. Two attributes are used more often than others and therefore have a special shortcut syntax: `id` and `class`.

Each element has a unique `id` attribute. JavaScript and CSS use this `id` to refer to the element. CSS uses the `class` attribute as a selector.

The syntax resembles the CSS syntax. To add `id`, append a hash and then `id`. For example, to assign `id sect1` to the `p` tag, you would write `p#sect1`. The template engine checks whether you have tried to assign `id` more than once. To add a class name, append a dot followed by the class name. For example, to assign the `important` class name to the `p` tag, you would write `p.important`.

You may also combine the syntax for the `id` and `class` attributes with the normal attribute syntax. Adding the `lang` attribute with the `en` value, you can write the `p` tag in one of the following ways:

```
p#sect1.important(lang='en')
p#sect1(class='important', lang='en')
p.important(id='sect1', lang='en')
p(id='sect1', class='important', lang='en')
```

> Note that it is currently not possible to spread the attributes across several lines.

If you use the syntax for the `id` or `class` name and omit the tag name, then the template engine generates a `div` tag:

```
#content
```

It translates into the following:

```
<div id="content"></div>
```

> The reason behind this shortcut syntax is that the `div` tags were a common choice when using HTML 4. When using HTML 5, there should be less of a need to use a `div` tag.

Localizing your website

You may want to translate your website into different languages. A common way to implement this is to derive the language of the website from the `Accept-Language` header attribute sent by the client browser. All the text content that should be translated is replaced by a message identifier. Based on the requested language, the message identifier is replaced with the text content. The template engine supports the standard GNU **gettext** `.po` files for this purpose. There are a lot of tools for this format that you can use if you need to localize a large website.

For the localization example, you will first create a new project with `dub`, as follows:

```
$ dub init localization --type=vibe.d
```

Using Templates for Your Web Pages

In the `index.dt` template file in the `views` folder, you will activate the text translation by appending `&` to the tag:

```
doctype html
head
    title& Localization example
body
    p& Welcome to our website
```

For each language, you will want to add a `.po` file. The file name must follow the `name.language_country.po` scheme. The name of this translation file is `name` and it is used in the following D code, `language` is an ISO 639-1 language code, and `country` is an ISO 3166-1 country code. Example file names are `example.en_US.po` for American English and `example.de_DE.po` for German.

The `.po` file contains the message identifier and translation. Here is the `example.en_US.po` file:

```
msgid "Localization example"
msgstr "Localization example"

msgid "Welcome to our website"
msgstr "Welcome to our website"
```

The following is the `example.de_DE.po` file:

```
msgid „Localization example"
msgstr „Lokalisierungsbeispiel"

msgid "Welcome to our website"
msgstr „Willkommen auf unsere Webseite"
```

> You can also use a short identifier instead of a sentence for the message identifier.

You should create a new `translations` folder and save the `.po` files in this folder.

[32]

The `.po` files are loaded as mixins at compile time. Therefore, the compiler must know where to find the files. Compilation of template files uses the same approach. In case of the templates files, the `views` folder is added as default path. You can specify the search path in the `dub.sdl` file by setting the `stringImportPaths` property. Just edit your `dub.sdl` file accordingly:

```
name "localization"
description "A simple vibe.d server application using a template with localization."
copyright "Copyright © 2015, PACKT Publishing"
authors "<your id>"
dependency "vibe-d" version="~>0.7.23"
versions "VibeDefaultMain"
stringImportPaths "views" "translations"
```

You have to specify all the folders that the compiler should search in. This also includes the `views` folder.

Now, the only missing piece is how to render the `index.dt` template file with the applied translations. It turns out that you have to provide some of your own utility functions. Localization is fully supported by the web framework that is described in *Chapter 4, Easy Forms with the Web Framework*. The following approach mimics the implementation in the web framework. You should place your code in the `app.d` file in the `source` folder, as shown in the following:

1. First, you should create a `TranslationContext` structure. This structure holds the information about the supported languages and strategy that is used to select the language for display:

    ```
    struct TranslationContext
    {
      import std.typetuple : TypeTuple;

      alias languages = TypeTuple!("en_US", "de_DE");
      mixin translationModule!"example";

      static string determineLanguage(HTTPServerRequest req)
      {
        import std.string : split, replace;

        auto acc_lang = "Accept-Language" in req.headers;
        if (acc_lang)
          return replace(split(*acc_lang, ",")[0], "-", "_");
        return null;
      }
    }
    ```

Using Templates for Your Web Pages

2. This structure uses some features unique to D. Again, scoped imports are used to import functions and types from the standard library. The list of languages is created as `TupleType`. This is basically a static list that is already known at compile time. The translation files are mixed in this `struct` with the help of the `translationModule` function. The `"example"` string is the first part of the name of the `.po` file. The `determineLanguage()` function defines which language to render. The strategy here is simple: if the client sends the header attribute that matches `Accept-Language`, then the first language in this list is returned, otherwise `null`. This can be improved; `Accept-Language` normally contains a list of languages. You have to compare this list with the list of languages that you support and choose the best match.

3. Next, you need to define a function that translates the template at compile time. The translation happens if you pass the special `diet_translate__()` function to the `render()` method as a template parameter. For each `id` message, the function is called and it returns the translated text. The `tr()` function translates an `id` message. It requires `TranslationContext` and the language provided as template parameters. If the client accepts only those languages that you do not support, then you can choose a default language; for example, the first language listed in the `TranslationContext` structure. The code looks similar to the following:

```
static string diet_translate__(string key, string
  context=null) {
  return tr!(TranslationContext,
    TranslationContext.languages[0])(key);
}
render!("index.dt", req, diet_translate__)(res);
```

4. For the supported languages, you have to solve the following problem: the `diet_translate__()` function is executed at compile time; however, the language chosen by the client is only available at run time. The solution is to create a `diet_translate__()` function for each supported language. To avoid a maintenance nightmare, you can use other unique D features; compile time reflection and code generation with mixins. Simply, enumerate the languages at compile time and insert the code for each language with a `mixin` statement. The whole `renderI18NTemplate()` function might look similar to this:

```
void renderI18NTemplate(string file)(HTTPServerRequest req,
  HTTPServerResponse res)
{
  switch (TranslationContext.determineLanguage(req)) {
    default:
```

[34]

Chapter 2

```
          static string diet_translate__(string key,
             string context=null) {
            return tr!(TranslationContext,
               TranslationContext.languages[0])(key);
          }
          render!(file, req, diet_translate__)(res);
          break;

       foreach (lang; TranslationContext.languages) {
          case lang:
            mixin("struct " ~ lang ~ " {
              static string diet_translate__(string key,
                 string context=null) {
                return tr!(TranslationContext, lang)(key); }
            }
            alias translate = " ~ lang ~ "
               .diet_translate__;");
            render!(file, req, translate)(res);
            break;
       }
     }
   }
```

5. Next, you need to define a utility function that only takes the filename as template parameter:

   ```
   HTTPServerRequestDelegate staticI18NTemplate(string file)()
   {
     return (HTTPServerRequest req, HTTPServerResponse res) {
       renderI18NTemplate!(file)(req, res);
     };
   }
   ```

6. Lastly, you should add the module constructor:

   ```
   shared static this()
   {
     auto settings = new HTTPServerSettings;
     settings.port = 8080;
     settings.bindAddresses = ["::1", "127.0.0.1"];
     listenHTTP(settings, staticI18NTemplate!"index.dt");

     logInfo("Please open http://127.0.0.1:8080/ in your
        browser.");
   }
   ```

Using Templates for Your Web Pages

Now, you are ready to compile and run your localization example. To see the various possible outputs, you have to change the list of languages in your browser. Select de_DE (German), first in the list, to see the German translation. Select any other language first in order to see the English translation.

The missing utility functions are the only reason why this example required a fair amount of coding. It is possible to generalize this approach to enable reuse. The `renderI18NTemplate()` and `staticI18NTemplate()` functions only depend on the `TranslationContext` structure. If you change the functions to accept the translation context type as a template parameter, then you can move both functions in another module and reuse this module in your other projects.

Adding D code to your template

Template files are processed at compile time; the template is turned into D code that outputs the resulting HTML code. If the user requests the page, then the HTML code is delivered with maximum speed as no additional processing is required. This differentiates vibe.d from other web frameworks, which either process a template file at the first or at every request. Of course, the processing time does not vanish, it is now a part of the compile time and slows down compilation speed.

This approach enables another useful feature. As a template is turned to D code, it is possible to embed the D code in the template. If a line starts with a dash (-), then the rest of the line is treated as a D statement. The statement is executed while delivering the page to the browser. The lines before the statement are already processed but not the lines after the statement. With this feature, it is possible to add dynamic elements to your template! There are two ways to output the result of a computation. If you append an equals sign (=) to a tag, then the template engine interprets the text that follows the tag as a D expression. If you omit the tag, then `div` is used automatically.

In a plain text, you can use string interpolation. You may place your D expression between the #{ and } symbols. The value of your expression is rendered at this position.

The following template file demonstrates the usage of embedded D code:

```
- import std.string : toUpper;
- string title = "Embedded D code example";
doctype html
head
  title= title.toUpper
body
  h1 #{ title }

  - foreach(i; 1..4)
```

```
    p This is paragraph #{i}

- int max(int a, int b)
  - if (a > b) return a; else return b;
p The maximum of 5 and 12 is #{ max(5, 12) }.
```

Note: Do not use { and } in your D code for grouping statements. If you need to define a function, then use the blocks from the template engine instead. For example, look at the `max()` function in the template example. As a general rule, you should avoid the definition of complex functions in a template. It is much easier and cleaner to create the function in a D module and then import the module. The preceding template shows this approach with the import of the `std.string` module too.

The output of = and #{ is escaped. If you need to use unescaped output, then you have to use the != and !{ symbols instead.

> Note that never trust the user input! Always validate and escape user input. If you do not follow these rules, then your website can be vulnerable to serious attacks, such as **Cross-site scripting (XSS)** and SQL injection. You can find more information about XSS at http://excess-xss.com/ and SQL injection at http://www.codeproject.com/Articles/9378/SQL-Injection-Attacks-and-Some-Tips-on-How-to-Prev. Both sites also describe how to prevent the attacks.

The D functions can be defined everywhere a tag is allowed. On using D functions, you can create parameterized, reusable blocks. This is very similar to using mixins of Jade. However, the Jade syntax for mixins is not supported by Diet templates.

Summary

You have learned about the Diet template engine that is integrated in the vibe.d framework. With this knowledge, you are already able to create large static websites. A real-world example is the vibe.d website at http://vibed.org/. You can find its source on GitHub at https://github.com/rejectedsoftware/vibed.org.

Note that most websites require some user interaction and change the page flow based on user input. In the next chapter, you will learn how to use forms and control the page flow. These topics are based on the knowledge that you already have about Diet templates.

3
Get Interactive – Forms and Flow Control

Users interact with web applications in many different ways, for example, browsing the site, playing audio and video, or entering data. In this chapter, forms are used to get user input and react to it. It explains how parameters are passed from the client side and accessed by the application. Routing and error page handlers are used for flow control.

In this chapter, you will learn the following:

- What are the different ways of form submission
- How the parameters are passed between client and server
- How to control the page flow with routing and the error page handler
- How to create a session
- How to upload and download files

Introducing the note application

In this chapter, you will be creating a simple web application: the note application. A note consists of a topic and content. Users can list, create, change, and delete notes. A note is stored with the creation time and can be marked as important. A file can be attached to a note. The users can only work with the notes that they have created.

Despite the fact that this is only a sample application, you should see the common patterns that are used here. A bug database requires the same user interactions. The basket of a web store has similar interactions. Even popular sites such as Facebook and YouTube use at least one of these interactions.

Get Interactive – Forms and Flow Control

In order to keep the implementation simple, the data is stored in the main memory. How to connect and use a database is covered in *Chapter 5, Accessing a Database*.

Creating a template with a simple form

Let's start with a web page to create a note. A simple design is as follows:

In HTML, there are two ways to submit a form: POST and GET. The difference is the way how the parameters are transferred to the server. In both cases, the browser issues an HTTP request. If you use the POST method, then the browser sends an HTTP request with the POST request method token to the server. The values of the form fields are transmitted in the request body. With the GET method, the browser sends a HTTP request with the GET request method token to the server. The values of the form fields are appended to the URL after a question mark (?) character.

> A **Uniform Resource Locator (URL)** describes the location of a resource that is available over the Internet. A typical URL looks similar to `http://www.example.com/path/to/file?user=yourid&action=create`. The parts of a URL are as follows:
> - `http://`: This denotes the protocol
> - `www.example.com`: This is the host name
> - `/path/to/file`: This is the path (or route in vibe.d) to a resource
> - `?user=yourid&action=create`: This is the query
> - `action=create`: This is a query field

Both the ways to submit are handled by vibe.d in a similar way. This will be true for your web application too. However, there are important differences between the two methods:

- The length of the URL is limited.
- `GET` is meant to retrieve data while `POST` is allowed to change the data.
- As a `GET` request only retrieves the data, the response may be cached. In general, this is not true for POST requests.

Let's take a closer look at these differences. RFC 7230 recommends that the length of the URL should not exceed 8.000 bytes. In reality, it is only safe to use URLs with a length of up to 2.000 bytes. If you need to send more data to the server, then you have to use the `POST` method to be on the safer side! A note can potentially be very long; therefore, you may want to use the `POST` method here. The semantic of the HTTP method is described in RFC 7231. The goal of the example application is to create a new note. The appropriate HTTP method is, therefore, the `POST` method. Nevertheless, the example application supports both the methods to demonstrate the uniform handling in the framework.

The `HTTPServerRequest` class represents the HTTP request. The request method is stored in the `method` public member. Members of interest are `HTTPMethod.GET` and `HTTPMethod.POST`. In the case of a POST request, the values of the form fields are stored in the `form` member. This member is of the `FormFields` type that you can use as an associative array. The URL parameters are stored in the `query` member that also is of the `FormFields` type.

From the previous chapters, you already know that the `URLRouter` class is used to connect a request URL with an action. Up till now, the action was to the render a static page. However, some data must be now processed if the user submits the form. A very basic type of processing is required to display the entered values on a new page. You can pass your local variables as template parameters to the `render!()` method. Then, you can access the variables in a template.

Get Interactive – Forms and Flow Control

Let's put all the pieces together, as shown in the following:

1. Create a new project with `dub`:

   ```
   $ dub init noteapp --type=vibe.d
   ```

2. Create a `create.dt` file in the `views` folder for the page with the web form. The input elements are named `form_topic` and `form_content`. The template code is as follows:

   ```
   doctype html
   head
     title Note app - Create a new note
     link(rel='stylesheet', type='text/css', href='note.css')
   body
     form(method='post',action='created')
       p
         label Topic
           input(name='form_topic',type='text',required)
       p
         label Content
           textarea(name='form_content')
       p
         button(type='reset') Reset
         button(type='submit') Create
   ```

3. The `created.dt` template in the same folder shows the entered values. Please note that this template refers to the `topic` and `content` variables and that the displayed text depends on the value of `content`:

   ```
   - import std.array: empty;
   doctype html
   head
     title Note app - Created a new note
     link(rel='stylesheet', type='text/css', href='note.css')
   body
     p You created a new note with topic '#{topic}'.
     - if (content.empty)
       p Content is empty.
     - else
       p Content is '#{content}'.
   ```

Chapter 3

4. You need to modify the generated D `app.d` module in the `source` folder. A new `createNote()` function extracts the values of the form fields via the names of the fields and passes them to the template. The `URLRouter` instance is set up to call this function in case of a POST request to the `/created` path:

```
import vibe.d;

shared static this()
{
  auto router = new URLRouter;
  router.get("/", staticTemplate!"create.dt");
  router.post("/created", &createNote);
  router.get("*", serveStaticFiles("public/"));

  auto settings = new HTTPServerSettings;
  settings.port = 8080;
  settings.bindAddresses = ["::1", "127.0.0.1"];
  listenHTTP(settings, router);

  logInfo("Please open http://127.0.0.1:8080/ in your
    browser.");
}

void createNote(HTTPServerRequest req,
                         HTTPServerResponse res)
{
  string topic = req.form.get("form_topic");
  string content = req.form.get("form_content");
  render!("created.dt", topic, content)(res);
}
```

You should run and modify the code by yourself!

What needs to be changed if you want to use an HTTP request with the GET request method token instead of the POST request method token? Clearly, you have to change `method` in the template:

```
form(method='get',action='/created')
```

You need to change the application too. The `URLRouter` instance must match the GET request:

```
router.get("/created", &createNote);
```

The `createNote()` function must use the `query` member, as follows:

```
void createNote(HTTPServerRequest req,
                         HTTPServerResponse res)
{
```

[43]

Get Interactive – Forms and Flow Control

```
      string topic = req.query.get("form_topic");
      string content = req.query.get("form_content");
      render!("created.dt", topic, content)(res);
}
```

If you run the modified version of the code, you should pay attention to how the form values are appended to the URL.

In fact, the code for using the GET method is nearly the same as the code for the POST method. The vibe.d framework hides most of the differences. It is even possible to support both methods in parallel. The HTTP method is defined as part of the form. In the D application, you can check the `method` member of `HTTPServerRequest` for the used HTTP method. As the route matching also considers the HTTP method, you have to register the route for both GET and POST method.

5. Modify the `create.dt` template file in order to contain two submit buttons. Add a `changeMethod()` JavaScript method to change the submit method based on the button. This requires the `myform` ID for the form. The method is called when the user clicks on one of the submit buttons:

```
doctype html
head
  title Note app - Create a new note
  link(rel='stylesheet', type='text/css', href='note.css')
  :javascript
    function changeMethod(m) {
      document.getElementById("myform").method = m;
    }
body
  form#myform(action='/created')
    p
      label Topic
        input(name='form_topic',type='text',required)
    p
      label Content
        textarea(name='form_content')
    p
      button(type='reset') Reset
      button(type='submit',onclick='changeMethod("post")')
        Create via POST
      button(type='submit',onclick='changeMethod("get")')
        Create via GET
```

6. As previously described, the application must now register the `createNote()` function to match GET and POST requests. Depending on the `method` member, the value of the form fields are retrieved from the `form` or `query` member. A new `reqmethod` local variable is used to hold the request method, which is also passed to the template:

   ```
   import vibe.d;

   shared static this()
   {
     auto router = new URLRouter;
     router.get("/", staticTemplate!"create.dt");
     router.get("/created", &createNote);
     router.post("/created", &createNote);
     router.get("*", serveStaticFiles("public/"));

     auto settings = new HTTPServerSettings;
     settings.port = 8080;
     settings.bindAddresses = ["::1", "127.0.0.1"];
     listenHTTP(settings, router);

     logInfo("Please open http://127.0.0.1:8080/ in your
       browser.");
   }

   void createNote(HTTPServerRequest req,
                   HTTPServerResponse res)
   {
     if (req.method != HTTPMethod.POST &&
       req.method != HTTPMethod.GET) return;
   auto formdata = (req.method == HTTPMethod.POST)
                       ? &req.form : &req.query;
     string topic = formdata.get("form_topic");
     string content = formdata.get("form_content");
     string reqmethod = httpMethodString(req.method);
     render!("created.dt", topic, content,
       reqmethod)(res); }
   ```

7. Finally, change the `created.dt` template to output the request method too. The request method is passed to the template as the `reqmethod` variable:

   ```
   - import std.array: empty;
   doctype html
   head
     title Note app - Created a new note
     link(rel='stylesheet', type='text/css', href='note.css')
   ```

```
body
  p You created a new note with topic '#{topic}'.
  - if (content.empty)
    p Content is empty.
  - else
    p Content is '#{content}'.
  p Request method: #{reqmethod}
```

A closer look at route matching

One of the key parts is the `URLRouter` class. You use this class to find a matching route and then run the action associated with this route. Matching follows these rules:

- Routes are compared in the order that they are initially specified.
- If a route matches, then the associate handler is executed.
- Matching stops if a handler writes a response.
- If no matching route is found, then the request is not handled. A 404 error is generated.

You need to specify the HTTP method and the route to match. The `match()` method takes the HTTP method, the match string, and the action callback as a parameter. The `get()`, `post()`, `put()`, `delete_()`, and `patch()` methods take only the match string and the action callback as a parameter and match the HTTP method of the same name. If you do not want to consider the HTTP method, then you use the `any()` method to add a match string. This can be useful if you want to log a request or implement some special route handling that is valid for all HTTP methods.

The match string may contain placeholders or wildcards. A wildcard is written as `*` and matches any character sequence. A placeholder starts with `:`, followed by the name of the placeholder. It ends with `/` or the end of the string. A placeholder matches only character sequences without `/`. The value of a placeholder can be looked up by the placeholder's name in the `param` member of the `HTTPServerRequest` class.

The action callback can be specified as a function, a delegate, or an object that implements the `HTTPServerRequestHandler` interface. In any case, the callback must take `HTTPServerRequest` and `HTTPServerResponse` as the parameters.

The design of route matching gives you a high degree of freedom. If you want to match the /note/create and /note/delete routes, then you can do it in the following ways:

- The `router.get("/note/create", &createNote);` and `router.get("/note/delete", &deleteNote);` code matches the route and run the appropriate action callback.
- The `router.get("/note/:action", &noteAction);` code matches every route starting with /note/, followed by exactly one string without /. The noteAction action callback can retrieve this part of the route with the name action from the params member of the request.
- The `router.get("/note/*", &noteAction);` code matches all the routes starting with /note/. To differentiate between different routes, the noteAction action callback has to look at the path member of the request.

If you add a lot of new routes, then you should call the rebuild() method to precompute the internal data structure for the purpose of matching. This forces an eager computation of the internal match structure. Otherwise, the computation is done when the first request happens that may delay the processing of the request.

There is no method to delete a route from an URLRouter instance. If you need to dynamically change routes, then there is an easy work-around for this limitation. Instead of using a single URLRouter instance for the whole application, you split your routes into groups and use an URLRouter instance for each group. Then, you install a dedicated URLRouter that forwards the requests using a catch-all route. A catch-all route only specifies the * wildcard to match every request:

```
// Container for the router instances
URLRouter[2] allrouters;

void setup()
{
  auto router = new URLRouter;

  // Create routers and register routes
  allrouters[0] = new URLRouter;
  allrouters[0].get( ... );
  allrouters[1] = new URLRouter;
  allrouters[1].get( ... );

  ...

  router.any("*", (req, res){
    foreach (r; allrouters)
```

[47]

```
      {
        r.handleRequest(req, res);
        if (res.headerWritten) return;
      }
    });

    listenHTTP(settings, router);
}
```

You can now easily change the `URLRouter` instances in the `allrouters` array, including adding new groups or removing the existing ones.

Serving static files

Static files such as the CSS stylesheet use a catch-all route in the note application:

```
router.get("*", serveStaticFiles("public/"));
```

All GET requests that are not previously handled are routed to the `serveStaticFiles()` function. This function sends the file to the client if it exists in the local `public/` folder. If the file is not found, then the function returns without writing a response. This is done for every request so the number of files and the content of the files may change during the lifetime of your application. You will only need to set up a route for GET requests as the browsers issues only HTTP GET requests for these files, in accordance with the semantic of the HTTP method explained earlier.

The `serveStaticFiles()` function itself checks whether the path in the request matches a configured prefix. The default value of the prefix is the root folder `/`. The prefix is removed from the request path. This relative path is appended to the local folder (which is the parameter to `serveStaticFiles()`) in order to form the local path of the file. With this approach, a flexible mapping from the request path to the local filesystem is possible.

As an example, you can use the `/static` path in the request and store the files in the local `public/` folder. An `HTTPFileServerSettings` object is required for the configuration:

- Change all references to the stylesheet in the template files to the following:

    ```
    link(rel='stylesheet', type='text/css', href='/static/note.css')
    ```

- Add the file server configuration to the `static this()` module constructor in the `app.d` D application:
  ```
  auto fileServerSettings = new HTTPFileServerSettings;
  fileServerSettings.serverPathPrefix = "/static/";
  ```

- The `serveStaticFiles()` function needs a second argument, as follows:
  ```
  router.get("*", serveStaticFiles("public/",
    fileServerSettings));
  ```

For the route matching, you can use the `*` or `/static/*` pattern. In the first case, the router unconditionally forwards all requests to the `serveStaticFiles()` function. In the second case, the router already does some filtering. In both cases, the function checks whether the request path has the required prefix.

The `HTTPFileServerSettings` class has an `options` member that allows more configurations:

- On setting `HTTPFileServerOption.failIfNotFound`, a 404 error response is generated if the requested file is not found. Use this option if you want to stop the routing in case a file is not found.
- If the request path is a folder and `HTTPFileServerOption.serveIndexHTML` is set, then `index.html` is appended to the path and this file is sent to the client, if it exists.

Use the `|` (binary or) operator if you want to set more than one option. For example, if you want to specify both options, you will write the following:

```
fileServerSettings.options =
  HTTPFileServerOption.failIfNotFound |
  HTTPFileServerOption.serveIndexHTML
```

The `maxAge` member controls the caching behavior of the browser. If the value is greater than 0 seconds, then the `Cache-Control` HTTP header field is added to the response. The browser will then cache this file to the specified number of seconds. This can greatly improve the response time if the file is requested for a second time.

The **Multipurpose Internet Mail Extensions (MIME)** type of the file is derived from the file extension. The list is hardcoded in the `getMimeTypeForFile()` public function.

If you have other special requirements, then you can use the `preWriteCallback` callback function to modify the response headers or perform some custom processing. Your changes are not validated by the framework, therefore, be careful!

Get Interactive – Forms and Flow Control

Let's illustrate a complex handling with a favicon. The favicon is a small image that the browser shows in the address bar, bookmark folder, and other places. Some information about the handling is as follows:

- If there is no `<link rel="icon" ...>` tag in the HTML file, then most browsers will request the `/favicon.ico` file. If serving of static files does not use the default `/` prefix, then special handling is required.
- While everybody (including vibe.d) uses `image/x-icon` as MIME type, the official registered MIME type is `image/vnd.microsoft.icon`. All major browsers support both the MIME types, therefore, it is safe to change the content type of the response.
- If the file is not found, then a 404 error should be returned.

To implement this, you will need the following special settings:

```
auto faviconSettings = new HTTPFileServerSettings;
faviconSettings.serverPathPrefix = "/";
faviconSettings.options = HTTPFileServerOption.failIfNotFound;
faviconSettings.preWriteCallback = (req, res, ref path) {
  res.headers["Content-Type"] = "image/vnd.microsoft.icon";
};
```

During setting up the router, you will need to add a match for `/favicon.ico`:

```
router.get("/favicon.ico", serveStaticFiles("public/",
  faviconSettings));
```

This finishes the setup of this special handling.

Storing session data

The note application is currently stateless. The entered data is displayed once and then it is lost. This is not useful. You need a place to store the data between requests. This place is the session. To use session, you have to instantiate `SessionStore` at server startup. A class implementing the `SessionStore` interface stores key/value pairs as an associative array. You start a session by calling the `startSession()` method of the response object and terminate a session with the `terminateSession()` method.

A cookie-based session is used by vibe.d. The session is available in the `session` member of the request if you previously called the `startSession()` method and if the client sends back a matching cookie.

The `SessionStore` is an interface. If you are only running a single instance of your vibe.d server, then you can use the simple `MemorySessionStore` implementation. If you use any kind of multiserver setup, then you need a persistent session store. The interface for the Redis database provides `RedisSessionStore` that can be used in this case.

> Do not store all of your data in the session. If your website has 1.000 concurrent sessions and each session is 10 MB in size, then your server requires 10 GB of main memory only to store the session data!

You can't store data types that are based on references in the session. This includes pointers and arrays of mutable types. However, you can store arrays of immutable types, for example, strings. The reason behind this restriction is that you cannot easily serialize and deserialize references. However, with immutable data types, it is possible to serialize the values without changing the semantic of the data structure. In general, this is a good thing as it prevents you to store all your data in the session and enables easy serialization to a database.

The note application does not use a database yet, so we need another solution. A global object can be used to encapsulate the data access. This object simple stores the data in an associative array. Later, this implementation can be changed to use a database.

Here is how you can use session:

1. In the `views` folder, create a `listnotes.dt` template that displays the topics of the current note. It also has the links to create a new note and log out:

    ```
    doctype html
    head
      title Note app - Create a new note
      link(rel='stylesheet', type='text/css', href='note.css')
    body
      p Your current notes
      - foreach (note; allnotes)
        p #{note.topic}
      a(href='create') Create a new note
      a(href='logout') Terminate session
    ```

2. In the `create.dt` template file, change the form tag to the following:

    ```
    form#myform(action='/note/create')
    ```

Get Interactive – Forms and Flow Control

3. The `app.d` application file in the `source` folder uses the `listnotes.dt` template to show the topics of all current notes. At first access, this creates the session object too. A click on the **create** link displays the `create.dt` template. After creating a new note, the `listnotes.dt` template is shown again, this time with the added topic. In order to store the data, a simple `NoteStore` object is used. Please note the use of the **Null Object Pattern** in the `NoteStore` implementation. In order to avoid checking for null references, an empty array, `empty`, is created. This array is returned if `NoteStore` contains no objects. This guarantees that the return value is never `null`, which simplifies clients of `NoteStore`:

```
import vibe.d;

shared static this()
{
  auto router = new URLRouter;
  router.get("/", &listNotes);
  router.get("/create", staticTemplate!"create.dt");
  router.get("/note/create", &createNote);
  router.post("/note/create", &createNote);
  router.get("/logout", &logout);
  router.get("*", serveStaticFiles("public/"));

  auto settings = new HTTPServerSettings;
  settings.sessionStore = new MemorySessionStore;
  settings.port = 8080;
  settings.bindAddresses = ["::1", "127.0.0.1"];
  listenHTTP(settings, router);

  logInfo("Please open http://127.0.0.1:8080/ in your
    browser.");
}

void logout(HTTPServerRequest req,
                   HTTPServerResponse res)
{
  noteStore.removeNotes(req.session.id);
  res.terminateSession();
  res.redirect("/");
}

void listNotes(HTTPServerRequest req,
                     HTTPServerResponse res)
{
```

Chapter 3

```
    if (!req.session) req.session = res.startSession();
    auto allnotes = noteStore.getNotes(req.session.id);
    render!("listnotes.dt", allnotes)(res);
}

void createNote(HTTPServerRequest req,
                        HTTPServerResponse res)
{
    if (req.method != HTTPMethod.POST &&
        req.method != HTTPMethod.GET) return;
    auto formdata = (req.method == HTTPMethod.POST)
        ? &req.form : &req.query;
    Note note;
    note.topic = formdata.get("form_topic");
    note.content = formdata.get("form_content");
    auto allnotes = noteStore.getNotes(req.session.id);
    allnotes ~= note;
    noteStore.setNotes(req.session.id, allnotes);
    res.redirect("/");
}

struct Note
{
    string topic;
    string content;
}

class NoteStore
{
    Note[][string] store;

    static Note[0] empty;

    Note[] getNotes(string id)
    {
        return (id in store) ? store[id] : empty;
    }

    void setNotes(string id, Note[] notes)
    {
        store[id] = notes;
    }

    void removeNotes(string id)
```

```
    {
      store.remove(id);
    }
  }
}

private __gshared NoteStore noteStore;

shared static this()
{
  noteStore = new NoteStore();
}
```

Please note that the `NoteStore` class has serious deficiencies; it has no synchronization to prevent race conditions and the data is not removed if the client does not close the session. A real solution has to use a database which is the topic of *Chapter 5, Accessing a Database*.

Authenticating the user

The notes that a user has entered should be private to this user. To implement this behavior, we need a way to authenticate a user and ensure that only the authenticated users can see their list of notes.

There are several methods available to authenticate a user. They all can be used with vibe.d:

- **Basic authentication**: The browser shows a pop-up window asking for a username and password. Both are transmitted in plaintext to the server.
- **Digest authentication**: The browser shows a pop-up window asking for a username and password. Only a digest of the password is transmitted to the server, not the password itself.
- **Form-based authentication**: The application itself embeds a form asking for a username and password. Both are transmitted in plaintext to the server.

It should be clear that a password must not be transmitted in plaintext over the wire. The use of TLS/SSL is mandatory in this case. How to configure vibe.d in order to use TLS/SSL is described in the *Form-based authentication* section.

In order to allow only the authenticated users to access a page, you use `URLRouter` again. A property of the route matching algorithm is to continue comparing, as long as no handler has written a response. This allows you to install a special handler that enforces the authenticated users, it is sometimes called a security interceptor. Set up a route that matches anything and check the provided credentials, for example, a username and password in the request. If the user is authenticated, then simply return. Otherwise, you can redirect to a login page or display an error.

With this approach, the security interceptor partitions your routes into two groups: the routes added before the security interceptor are accessible for everyone and the routes after the security interceptor are accessible only for authenticated users.

Using basic authentication

The provided `performBasicAuth()` and `performDigestAuth()` functions work as the security interceptors. To use form-based authentication, you have to develop your own handler. Adding basic authentication is straightforward. All you need to provide is a delegate that checks the username and password and the realm (a string describing the site that requests the authentication). A welcome `index.dt` page is added that links to the `listnotes.dt` page. Routing is set up to allow everybody to view the welcome page and static files, but everything else requires an authenticated user. Here is how to add basic authentication to the note application:

1. Add a welcome `index.dt` page in the `views` folder. It has a link to a protected page that triggers the authentication:

    ```
    doctype html
    head
      title Note app
      link(rel='stylesheet', type='text/css', href='/static/note.css')
    body
      h1 Welcome to the Note app
      p Please <a href="/listnotes">login</a> to view your notes.
    ```

2. The application itself requires some changes. First, add a method to verify the username and password:

    ```
    bool checkPassword(string user, string password)
    {
       return user == "yourid" && password =="secret";
    }
    ```

Get Interactive – Forms and Flow Control

3. The `static this()` module constructor must set up the authentication. The new template requires small changes to the routing. Please note the catch-all route that performs the user authentication:

   ```
   shared static this()
   {
     auto fileServerSettings = new HTTPFileServerSettings;
     fileServerSettings.serverPathPrefix = "/static/";

     auto router = new URLRouter;
     router.get("/", staticTemplate!"index.dt");
     router.get("/static/*", serveStaticFiles("public/",
       fileServerSettings));
     router.any("*", performBasicAuth("The Note app",
       toDelegate(&checkPassword)));
     router.get("/listnotes", &listNotes);
     router.get("/create", staticTemplate!"create.dt");
     router.get("/note/create", &createNote);
     router.post("/note/create", &createNote);
     router.get("/logout", &logout);

     auto settings = new HTTPServerSettings;
     settings.sessionStore = new MemorySessionStore;
     settings.port = 8080;
     settings.bindAddresses = ["::1", "127.0.0.1"];
     listenHTTP(settings, router);

     logInfo("Please open http://127.0.0.1:8080/ in your
       browser.");
   }
   ```

4. Another required change is that the `createNote()` function redirects to /listnotes instead of the welcome page:

   ```
   void createNote(HTTPServerRequest req,
     HTTPServerResponse res)
   {
     ...
     res.redirect("/listnotes");
   }
   ```

If you start the application and click on the **login** link, then your browser will display a popup asking for a username and password:

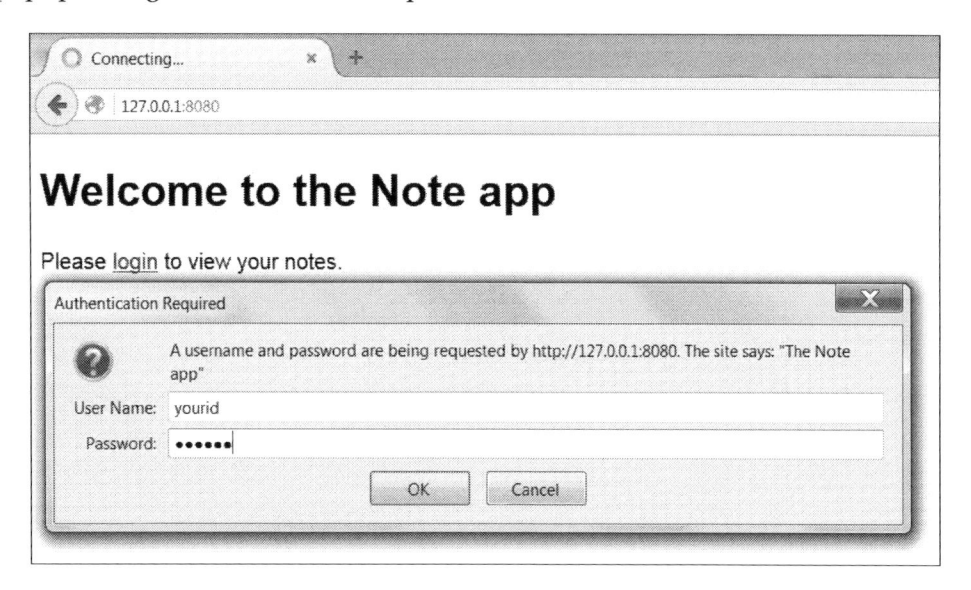

Using digest authentication

Based on this version, you can also support digest authentication. The main difference is that only a hash of the password is transmitted to the client. This requires a different method to verify the password. A possibility is to create a password file with the `htdigest` utility and read it in your application and use the hashes in this file. If the plain text passwords are known, then the digest can be created with the `createDigestPassword()` function:

```
string digestPassword(string realm, string user)
{
  if (realm =="The Note app" && user == "yourid")
    return createDigestPassword(realm, user, "secret");
  return "";
}
```

Get Interactive – Forms and Flow Control

The setup requires an additional object of the `DigestAuthInfo` class as some additional information must be stored. It is also used for the realm (the site description that is displayed to the user). In the `static this()` module constructor, the `DigestAuthInfo` object is created and the call to `performBasicAuth()` is replaced with a call to `performDigestAuth()`:

```
shared static this()
{
  auto authinfo = new DigestAuthInfo;
  authinfo.realm = "The Note app";

  auto fileServerSettings = new HTTPFileServerSettings;
  fileServerSettings.serverPathPrefix = "/static/";

  auto router = new URLRouter;
  router.get("/", staticTemplate!"index.dt");
  router.get("/static/*", serveStaticFiles("public/",
    fileServerSettings));
  router.any("*", performDigestAuth(authinfo,
    toDelegate(&digestPassword)));
  router.get("/listnotes", &listNotes);
  router.get("/create", staticTemplate!"create.dt");
  router.get("/note/create", &createNote);
  router.post("/note/create", &createNote);
  router.get("/logout", &logout);

  auto settings = new HTTPServerSettings;
  settings.sessionStore = new MemorySessionStore;
  settings.port = 8080;
  settings.bindAddresses = ["::1", "127.0.0.1"];
  listenHTTP(settings, router);

  logInfo("Please open http://127.0.0.1:8080/ in your browser.");
}
```

The browser shows the same popup with the basic authentication. The difference between basic and digest authentication is not visible to the user.

Form-based authentication

The disadvantage of basic and digest authentication is that you have no control over the popup that is displayed by the browser. This is only possible if you create your own web form. Besides this form, you need a way to ensure that only the authenticated users see the protected pages. Here is a way to achieve this goal:

- A successful login starts a session. A flag indicating the user was authenticated is stored in the session data. For information purpose, the username is also stored.
- A security interceptor is installed that checks whether a session exists with an authenticated user. In this case, nothing happens. Otherwise, a redirect to the login page is created.
- On logout, the flag indicating the user was authenticated is cleared and the session is terminated.

Only small changes to the application are required, as follows:

1. Replace the content of `index.dt` with a login form:

```
doctype html
head
  title Note app
  link(rel='stylesheet', type='text/css', href='/static/note.css')
body
  h1 Welcome to the Note app
  form(method='get',action='/login')
    fieldset
      legend Please login to view your notes
      p
        label(for='username') User
        input(name='username',type='text',required)
      p
        label(for='password') Password
        input(name='password',type='password',required)
      p
        button(type='reset') Reset
        button(type='submit') Login
```

Get Interactive – Forms and Flow Control

2. In the `app.d` application module, define a `User` structure for the session data:

   ```
   struct User
   {
     bool loggedIn;
     string name;
   }
   ```

3. The `login()` function retrieves the username and password from the form data and verifies them. On success, a session is started and a `User` structure is stored in the session:

   ```
   void login(HTTPServerRequest req, HTTPServerResponse res)
   {
     if (req.method != HTTPMethod.POST &&
         req.method != HTTPMethod.GET) return;
     auto formdata = (req.method == HTTPMethod.POST)
       ? &req.form : &req.query;
     string username = formdata.get("username");
     string password = formdata.get("password");
     if (username == "yourid" && password == "secret")
     {
       if (!req.session)
         req.session = res.startSession();

       User user;
       user.loggedIn = true;
       user.name = username;
       req.session.set!User("user", user);
       res.redirect("/listnotes");
     }
     res.redirect("/");
   }
   ```

4. The `logout()` function clears the session data:

   ```
   void logout(HTTPServerRequest req,
               HTTPServerResponse res)
   {
     req.session.set!User("user", User.init);
     noteStore.removeNotes(req.session.id);
     res.terminateSession();
     res.redirect("/");
   }
   ```

5. The security interceptor checks for a session and the `loggedIn` flag:
    ```
    void ensureAuth(HTTPServerRequest req,
      HTTPServerResponse res)
    {
      if (req.session)
      {
        auto user = req.session.get!User("user");
        if (user.loggedIn) return ;
      }
      res.redirect("/");
    }
    ```

6. Lastly, you need to add the `login()`, `logout()`, and `ensureAuth()` functions to router in the `static this()` module constructor:
    ```
    shared static this()
    {
      auto fileServerSettings = new
        HTTPFileServerSettings;
      fileServerSettings.serverPathPrefix = "/static/";

      auto router = new URLRouter;
      router.get("/", staticTemplate!"index.dt");
      router.get("/login", &login);
      router.get("/static/*",
        serveStaticFiles("public/",
        fileServerSettings));
      router.any("*", &ensureAuth);
      router.get("/listnotes", &listNotes);
      router.get("/create", staticTemplate!"create.dt");
      router.get("/note/create", &createNote);
      router.post("/note/create", &createNote);
      router.get("/logout", &logout);

      auto settings = new HTTPServerSettings;
      settings.sessionStore = new MemorySessionStore;
      settings.port = 8080;
      settings.bindAddresses = ["::1", "127.0.0.1"];
      listenHTTP(settings, router);

      logInfo("Please open http://127.0.0.1:8080/ in your
        browser.");
    }
    ```

[61]

Get Interactive – Forms and Flow Control

How secure is the form-based authentication? It should be clear that the connection should be encrypted in order to protect the password. The `ensureAuth()` security interceptor ensures that only the authenticated users can access the protected pages. However, this does not help against replay attacks. Encrypting the connection helps again. The conclusion is that you should always use TLS/SSL with the form-based authentication.

Enabling TLS/SSL with your application

To use TLS/SSL, you need a server certificate for your web server. This server certificate must be signed by a **certification authority** (**CA**) in order to be accepted by the browser. Unfortunately, most server certificates cost a lot of money, especially for commercial use. However, for the purpose of testing, you can create a self-signed certificate. The browser will then complain that the certificate is not valid but will still encrypt the connection.

> Do not use a self-signed certificate in a production environment. A visitor of your website cannot check the validity of the certificate.

A self-signed certificate can be created with **OpenSSL**. Just type the following on a command line:

```
$ openssl req -x509 -newkey rsa:2048 -keyout key.pem -out cert.pem -days 3650 -nodes
Generating a 2048 bit RSA private key
...............+++
........+++
writing new private key to 'key.perm'
-----
You are about to be asked to enter information that will be incorporated
into your certificate request.
What you are about to enter is what is called a Distinguished Name or a DN.
There are quite a few fields but you can leave some blank
For some fields there will be a default value,
If you enter '.', the field will be left blank.
-----
Country Name (2 letter code) [AU]: DE
State or Province Name (full name) [Some-State]:
```

```
Locality Name (eg, city) []: Duesseldorf
Organization Name (eg, company) [Internet Widgits Pty Ltd]:
Organizational Unit Name (eg, section) []:
Common Name (e.g. server FQDN or YOUR name) []: localhost
Email Address []:
```

With a real certificate, the common name must match the hostname of your website.

The command creates two files, the `key.perm` private key file and the `cert.perm` certificate file. Both files are required by vibe.d to set up TLS/SSL. In order to enable TLS/SSL for your website, you have to add the following lines in the `static this()` constructor:

```
auto settings = new HTTPServerSettings;
// ...
settings.sslContext = createSSLContext(SSLContextKind.server);
settings.sslContext.useCertificateChainFile("cert.pem");
settings.sslContext.usePrivateKeyFile("key.pem");
listenHTTP(settings, router);
```

If you now open the browser at `https://127.0.0.1:8080`, then a warning is displayed stating that the certificate of the website is not valid. You need to confirm that you accept the risk and want to continue. Then, the welcome page is displayed; however, this time, using an encrypted connection.

Displaying an error page

If the server detects an error condition during processing of a request, then the response contains a status code indicating the cause of the error. Common status codes are 404 if a page is not found and 401 if the client is not authorized.

Then, the browser displays an error page describing the error. However, it is also possible to send an HTML page, together with the status code. To enable this feature, you need to provide an `HTTPServerErrorPageHandler` delegate. This handler can then, for example, render a template.

You can create a small application to demonstrates this, as shown in the following:

1. Create a new project with `dub`:

    ```
    $ dub init errorpage --type=vibe.d
    ```

Get Interactive – Forms and Flow Control

2. Create a `index.dt` template in the `views` folder. It contains a link to a non-existent page:

   ```
   doctype html
   head
     title Error page demonstration
   body
     p Click on the <a href="/notfound">link</a> to generate a
       404 error.
   ```

3. Create a `error.dt` template in the `views` folder. This will display information about the error. The template expects two parameters:

   ```
   doctype html
   head
     title An error occured
   body
     p An error occured!
     p The requested path: #{req.path}
     p The status code: #{error.code}
     p The error message: #{error.message}
   ```

4. Add the error page handler to the `app.d` application in the `source` folder:

   ```
   import vibe.d;

   shared static this()
   {
     auto router = new URLRouter;
     router.get("/", staticTemplate!"index.dt");

     auto settings = new HTTPServerSettings;
     settings.errorPageHandler = toDelegate(&errorPage);
     settings.port = 8080;
     settings.bindAddresses = ["::1", "127.0.0.1"];
     listenHTTP(settings, router);

     logInfo("Please open http://127.0.0.1:8080/ in your
       browser.");
   }

   void errorPage(HTTPServerRequest req,
                  HTTPServerResponse res,
                  HTTPServerErrorInfo error)
   {
     render!("error.dt", req, error)(res);
   }
   ```

Chapter 3

If you start this application and click on the link, then your error page is displayed. Even if an error occurred, you are now able to display a nice page to the user.

Uploading files

Some applications allow the user to upload files. Even for the note application, it might be useful to attach a file to a note. To upload a file, you integrate an input field of the `file` type into your form. If you submit the form, then the form data and the file must be transmitted to the server. You need to use the POST method and the `multipart/form-data` encoding to make this work. On the server side, the `files` member contains the original filename and the path of the uploaded file. The member works as an associative array. The key is the name of the input field in the form.

Let's create an application to demonstrate this, as shown in the following:

1. Create a new project with `dub`:

    ```
    $ dub init upload --type=vibe.d
    ```

2. Create a `index.dt` template in the `views` folder. It contains a simple form with an input field to select a file:

    ```
    doctype html
    head
      title File upload
    body
      form(method='post',action='/upload',enctype='multipart/form-data')
        p
          label(for='filename') File
          input(name='filename',type='file',required)
        p
          button(type='reset') Reset
          button(type='submit') Upload
    ```

3. The `app.d` application only moves the uploaded file to the current path of the server using the `moveFile()` function. Due to filesystem restrictions, this only works if the uploaded file and the current path are in the same hard disk partition. If this is not the case, then the `moveFile()` function throws an exception. In this case, the file is not moved but copied with the `copyFile()` function:

    ```
    import vibe.d;

    shared static this()
    {
    ```

[65]

```d
auto router = new URLRouter;
router.get("/", staticTemplate!"index.dt");
router.post("/upload", &upload);

auto settings = new HTTPServerSettings;
settings.port = 8080;
settings.bindAddresses = ["::1", "127.0.0.1"];
listenHTTP(settings, router);

logInfo("Please open http://127.0.0.1:8080/ in your
   browser.");
}

void upload(HTTPServerRequest req,
            HTTPServerResponse res)
{
   auto f = "filename" in req.files;
   try
      moveFile(f.tempPath, Path(".") ~ f.filename);
   catch (Exception e)
      copyFile(f.tempPath, Path(".") ~ f.filename);
   res.redirect("/");
}
```

Uploading files can be dangerous. If you use this in a real application, you should check the filename for invalid characters. You should also add a size limit to the input field. Currently, vibe.d does not restrict the size of uploaded files. Therefore, the /tmp folder that is used by vibe.d to temporarily store the uploaded file should be on a separate partition in order to avoid using all the free space on the filesystem in case of an attack.

Summary

Web forms are an important way to interact with a user. In this chapter, you learned how to process forms. You applied your knowledge about Diet templates from the previous chapter and extended it with passing of local variables to the template. Routing of requests played an important role in order to navigate to different pages. You learned about the different ways to authenticate a user and how to work with sessions.

The next chapter introduces the web framework. This framework abstracts from all the details of form handling and makes creating an HTML application very easy.

4
Easy Forms with the Web Framework

The web framework for HTML clients is used to work easily with forms. It makes building a web application really simple.

In this chapter, we will cover the following topics:

- Using a web framework to create web applications
- Validating user input
- Implementing security with the `@before` attribute
- Localizing your web content

Taking advantage of unique D features

In the previous chapters, each application initialized routes and associated them with the handler functions or delegates. There are two shortcomings: you have to type a lot, and there is a certain distance between the places where the route is initialized and the handler is defined.

For sure, we can do better. Let's assume that the handler functions are all methods of an object:

```
class WebApp
{
  void getIndex(HTTPServerRequest req, HTTPServerResponse res)
  { /* ... */ }

  void postNote(HTTPServerRequest req, HTTPServerResponse res)
  { /* ... */ }
}
```

Easy Forms with the Web Framework

Then, you can perform the following functions:

- The route and HTTP method can be derived from the method name
- User-defined attributes can be used to associate a route with a method, set up an error handler, require authentication, and so on

This is possible with D at compile time! With compile-time reflection, you can enumerate all the methods of an object. Then, you can derive a route from the method name and initialize the route. Here is the basic coding of the idea:

```d
void register(T : Object)(T o)
{
  import std.uni: toLower;

  auto router = new URLRouter;

  foreach (memberName; __traits(allMembers, T))
  {
    alias helper(alias U) = U;
    alias member = helper!(__traits(getMember, o,
      memberName));
    static if (is(typeof(member) == function)
        && __traits(getProtection, member) == "public")
    {
      static if (memberName.length > 3
          && memberName[0..3] == "get")
      {
        enum route = "/" ~ toLower(memberName[3..$]);
        router.get(route,
            &__traits(getMember, o, memberName));
      }
      else static if (memberName.length > 4
          && memberName[0..4] == "post")
      {
        enum route = "/" ~ toLower(memberName[4..$]);
        router.post(route,
            &__traits(getMember, o, memberName));
      }
    }
  }
}
```

Using the template type specialization, `T : object`, this template function can be instantiated only for the `class` and `interface` types. The function loops over all the member names of the `T` class, which you retrieve with `__traits(allMembers, T)`. The member itself is retrieved with `__traits(getMember, o, memberName)`. Only public methods are candidates to register as a route handler. The `is(typeof(member) == function` makes sure that the member is a method and `__traits(getProtection, member) == "public"` checks the protection level. If a method name starts with `get`, then this method is used as a handler for HTTP GET requests. The route is the method name without `get`; the `getIndex()` method is the handler for the `/index` route. The same algorithm is used for `post`.

The new `register()` function is used during initialization:

```
shared static this()
{
  auto app = new WebApp;
  register(app);
  /* ... */
}
```

The source that you have to type to initialize the routes is really reduced. As the `register()` function is executed at compile time, the loop in the function is unrolled, and the object code generated for this call is a sequence of calls to `router.get()` and `router.post()`. There is no runtime overhead with this approach!

This is the basic idea of the web framework. The actual implementation is much more complex. For example, the preceding `register()` function fails if the class contains the `static` methods and does not support annotations.

Converting the note application

Let's use the web framework to implement the note application introduced in the previous chapter.

Naming the handler functions

The handler functions become methods of a new `NoteApplication` class. The HTTP method is derived from the prefix of the method name as follows:

HTTP method	Prefixes
GET	`get`, `query`, `getter @property` methods, and methods named `index`
POST	`post`, `create`, `add`, and no prefix

Easy Forms with the Web Framework

HTTP method	Prefixes
PUT	`put`, `set`, and setter `@property` methods
PATCH	`patch` and `update`
DELETE	`delete`, `erase`, and `remove`

Only the `GET` and `POST` methods are usually used in web applications, but you should know all the prefixes in order to avoid surprises. The prefix is stripped from the name to form the route.

You can use the `@path` and `@method` annotations to specify a different route and HTTP method. The following is an example:

```
@method(HTTPMethod.GET)
@path("logout")
void leave() { /* ... */ }
```

This overrides the default `POST` method with `GET` and changes the URL path from `/leave` to `/logout`.

Passing values of form fields

The web framework automatically binds values of form fields to the parameter names of handler functions. Basically, if the parameter name does not start with an underscore, then the value of the form field with the same name is bound to this parameter. If the form field is missing, then this results in a runtime exception.

You are not restricted to the `string` parameters. The vibe.d framework supports type conversion, too. Here are the rules:

- If the type of the parameter is an array type, then the values of form fields with the `<parameter name>_<index>` name are mapped to the array, where `<index>` denotes the zero-based index of the element in the array. The framework searches in ascending order for the first index number for which no form field exists. This index number is the length of the array.

- Struct types support two different ways of mapping. If the struct has a `fromString()` or `fromStringValidate()` method, then this method is called. Otherwise, each struct member is bound to the value of a form field with the `<parameter name>_<member_name>` name.

- The parameter is optional if the type is `Nullable!T` or has a default value. All the other parameters are required.

- A `bool` parameter is set to `true` if the form field is present and `false` otherwise. This can be used for HTML checkboxes.

- For all the other types, a conversion function is called to convert the string value of the form field to the parameter type. The following functions are tried in this order: a static `fromStringValidate()` method, static `fromString()` method, and `std.conv.to!T` method.
- All the rules are applied recursively to support nested types.

If the parameter type is `HTTPServerRequest` or `HTTPServerResponse`, then the parameter receives the corresponding objects from the current request.

Creating sessions and session variables

The note application uses a session to store an identifier that is used to look up all the notes in `NoteStore`. The web framework supports session variables with the `SessionVar!()` struct. A session variable is declared as a member of the web application class:

```
private SessionVar!(string, "uuid") uuid;
```

The first template parameter is the type of the session variable, and the second is the name in the session store.

> Two different variables with the same name are mapped to the same value!

A session is automatically started the first time a session variable is set. To terminate a session, you just call `terminateSession()`.

Putting everything together

With the information about the web framework at hand, you can now create the application:

1. Create a new project with `dub`, using the following command:

    ```
    $ dub init noteapp --type=vibe.d
    ```

2. You need to modify the generated D `app.d` module in the `source` folder with the following content:

    ```
    import vibe.d;

    class NoteApplication
    {
    ```

Easy Forms with the Web Framework

```d
    private SessionVar!(string, "uuid") uuid;

    struct FormData
    {
      string topic;
      string content;
    }

    void index()
    {
      import std.uuid : randomUUID;

      if (uuid == null) uuid = randomUUID.toString;
      auto allnotes = noteStore.getNotes(uuid);
      render!("listnotes.dt", allnotes);
    }

    @method(HTTPMethod.GET)
    void logout()
    {
      terminateSession();
      redirect("/");
    }

    void getNoteEntry()
    {
      render!("create.dt");
    }

    void createNewNote(FormData form)
    {
      Note note;
      note.topic = form.topic;
      note.content = form.content;
      auto allnotes = noteStore.getNotes(uuid);
      allnotes ~= note;
      noteStore.setNotes(uuid, allnotes);
      redirect("/");
    }
}

shared static this()
{
  auto router = new URLRouter;
```

[72]

```d
    router.registerWebInterface(new NoteApplication);

    auto settings = new HTTPServerSettings;
    settings.sessionStore = new MemorySessionStore;
    settings.port = 8080;
    settings.bindAddresses = ["::1", "127.0.0.1"];
    listenHTTP(settings, router);

    logInfo("Please open http://127.0.0.1:8080/ in your
       browser.");
}

struct Note
{
  string topic;
  string content;
}

class NoteStore
{
  Note[][string] store;

  static Note[0] empty;

  Note[] getNotes(string id)
  {
    return (id in store) ? store[id] : empty;
  }

  void setNotes(string id, Note[] notes)
  {
    store[id] = notes;
  }

  void removeNotes(string id)
  {
    store.remove(id);
  }
}

private __gshared NoteStore noteStore;

shared static this()
{
  noteStore = new NoteStore();
}
```

Easy Forms with the Web Framework

3. In the `views` folder, create a `listnotes.dt` template, which displays the topics of the current note:

   ```
   doctype html
   head
     title Note app - Create a new note
     link(rel='stylesheet', href='note.css')
   body
     p Your current notes
     - foreach (note; allnotes)
       p #{note.topic}
     a(href='note_entry') Create a new note
     a(href='logout') Terminate session
   ```

4. Create a `create.dt` file in the `views` folder for the page with the web form:

   ```
   doctype html
   head
     title Note app - Create a new note
     link(rel='stylesheet', href='note.css')
   body
     form(method='post',action='/new_note')
       fieldset
         legend Your new note
         p
           label(for='form_topic') Topic
           input(name='form_topic',type='text',required)
         p
           label(for='form_content') Content
           textarea(name='form_content',rows='5',cols='40')
         p
           button(type='reset') Reset
           button(type='submit') Create
   ```

The `NoteApplication` class uses most of the framework features discussed in the previous sections. The source code is now more compact, and a lot of the technical details such as request and response classes are gone. The web framework enables you to focus on the functionality of your application, accelerating your web development.

Validating user input

With the use of the web framework, the application implicitly checks that the form fields for the topic and content text are present. The check happens at the time the framework populates the `FormData` struct with the values of the form fields. There is no way to display this error yet. If you remove one of the form fields and run the application, then the application seems to crash. As the same approach is used to validate user input, we need to fix this.

Displaying error messages with @errorDisplay

If an error occurs, then a web page must be rendered to show the error message. You use the `@errorDisplay` annotation to define the function to be called in order to display the error:

```
@errorDisplay!getError
void createNewNote(FormData form) { /* ... */ }
```

The `getError()` method takes a `_error` parameter, which receives information about the error. In the simplest cases, the type of the parameter is `string` and contains an error message. Note the underscore in the parameter name: because of this, the parameter is not bound to the value of a form field. You can use a template to display the error message, but let's write the message only. An `HTTPServerResponse` object is needed for this:

```
void getError(string _error = null, HTTPServerResponse res)
{
  res.writeBody(_error);
}
```

If you remove the `form_content` input field in the `create.dt` template now and then run the application, the **Missing parameter form_content** error message is displayed.

To be useful for user input validation, this basic error handling must be extended. Normally, the error message is shown on the same page near the input field. To show the error message on the same page, you need to call the `getNoteEntry()` method. Now the `_error` parameter is passed as well:

```
void getNoteEntry(string _error = null)
{
  render!("create.dt", _error);
}
```

[75]

Easy Forms with the Web Framework

The `create.dt` template needs to display the error message, if present:

```
doctype html
head
  title Note app - Create a new note
  link(rel='stylesheet', type='text/css', href='note.css')
body
  form(method='post',action='/new_note')
    fieldset
      legend Your new note
      p
        label(for='form_topic') Topic
        input(name='form_topic',type='text',required)
      p
        label(for='form_content') Content
        textarea(name='form_content',rows='5',cols='40')
      p
        button(type='reset') Reset
        button(type='submit') Create
    - if (_error)
        p(style='color: red')= _error
```

A possible user input validation is that the topic string should have at least three characters. All you need to do is check the string length and throw an exception if the string is too short:

```
@errorDisplay!getNoteEntry
void createNewNote(FormData form)
{
  Note note;
  note.topic = form.topic;
  note.content = form.content;
  if (note.topic.length < 3)
    throw new Exception("Topic must have at least 3 chars");
  auto allnotes = noteStore.getNotes(uuid);
  allnotes ~= note;
  noteStore.setNotes(uuid, allnotes);
  redirect("/");
}
```

If you compile and run this application, you will see an error message if you enter less than three characters for the topic.

What is still missing is some information about the form field causing the validation error. You define a new exception class to capture this information:

```
class ValidationException : Exception
{
  string field;

  this(string msg, string field)
  {
    super(msg);
    this.field = field;
  }
}
```

The value of the `field` member must also be passed to the `getNodeEntry()` method. Therefore, you change the type of _error to `Exception`. To access the field member, you must use a cast: `(cast(ValidationException) _error).field`.

Refining the validation

While the approach from the previous section works, there is a better solution. If the framework cannot assign a form field value to a parameter, then an exception is raised. The exception and name of the offending parameter (not the form field!) are passed to the function, which constructs the value of the _error parameter. If the type of _error is `struct` with two string members, then the parameter name is assigned to the second member. A possible definition is as follows:

```
struct ValidationErrorData
{
  string msg;
  string field;
}
```

The signature of `getNoteEntry()` is changed to the following:

```
void getNoteEntry(ValidationErrorData _error =
  ValidationErrorData.init)
{
  render!("create.dt", _error);
}
```

Easy Forms with the Web Framework

The type conversion step can automatically provide the parameter name. Remember that a type conversion method is called if the parameter type is `struct`. All you need to do is wrap your parameter with `struct` and do the validation in the `fromStringValidate()` or `fromString()` method. Here is a possible validation for the topic string:

```
struct ValidTopic
{
  private string value;

  private this(string value) { this.value = value; }
  @disable this();

  string toString() const pure nothrow @safe { return value; }
  alias toString this;

  static Nullable!ValidTopic fromStringValidate(string str,
    string* error)
  {
    // work around disabled default construction
    Nullable!ValidTopic ret =
      Nullable!ValidTopic(ValidTopic(null));
    ret.nullify();

    if (str.length < 3)
        *error = "Must have at least 3 characters";
    else
        ret = ValidTopic(str);
    return ret;
  }
}
```

> Note the use of the `Nullable` template. A `Nullable!T` object has a new distinctive `null` state. The framework uses this to check whether a value was assigned or not, independent of the type of the value.

The `ValidTopic` struct holds a string value. The only way to create an instance of this struct is with the `fromStringValidate()` method, which also performs the validation. If the validation fails, then the error message is set and a null instance is returned. The `createNewNote()` method now uses the `ValidTopic` type for the parameter:

```
@errorDisplay!getNoteEntry
void createNewNote(ValidTopic form_topic, string form_content)
{
  Note note;
  note.topic = form_topic;
  note.content = form_content;
  auto allnotes = noteStore.getNotes(uuid);
  allnotes ~= note;
  noteStore.setNotes(uuid, allnotes);
  redirect("/");
}
```

The `FormData` struct is not used here. You could also change the `topic` type of member in `FormData` to `ValidTopic`. As the parameter mapping rules are applied recursively, the validation method is called. However, now the parameter name denotes the whole `FormData` struct and you need another solution to relate the error message with the input field.

The last step is to display the error message. There are now several places where an error message can be displayed. If a validation fails, then the field is known and the error message can be displayed near the input field. If an exception occurs during the execution of the handler method, then the `field` member is empty. The error message should be displayed in a status section. The code to generate the message is put in the `showerror()` function. The `create.dt` template will look as follows:

```
- void showerror(string field = null)
  - if (_error.msg && _error.field == field)
      p(style='color: red')= _error.msg
doctype html
head
  title Note app - Create a new note
  link(rel='stylesheet', href='note.css')
body
  form(method='post',action='/new_note')
    fieldset
      legend Your new note
      p
        label(for='form_topic') Topic
```

```
            input(name='form_topic',type='text',required)
            - showerror("form_topic");
        p
            label(for='form_content') Content
            textarea(name='form_content',rows='5',cols='40')
            - showerror("form_content");
        p
            button(type='reset') Reset
            button(type='submit') Create
    - showerror();
```

The `vibe.d` framework already provides you with the following validation structs:

- `ValidEmail`: Checks the syntax of an e-mail address.
- `ValidUsername` and `ValidPassword`: Checks whether the passed strings meet certain criteria commonly applied to the username and password. This includes the minimal and maximal length and use of special characters.
- `Confirm!param`: Checks whether the parameter value matches the value of the `param` parameter.

There also exist low-level methods (`validateEmail()`, `validateUserName()`, `validateIdent()`, `validatePassword()`, and `validateString()`), which you can use to build your own validation structs.

Adding authentication

Our note application currently does not authenticate the user. In *Chapter 3, Get Interactive – Forms and Flow Control*, you learned how to enforce authentication by setting up a security interceptor. With the use of the web framework, the routes are automatically created and there is no way to insert a security interceptor. You could split your application class into a class containing only the unsecured functionality and another class containing the secured functionality. It is possible to install a security interceptor between the calls to `registerWebInterface()`. The drawback is that you now have two classes.

An elegant way to solve this problem would be to annotate all the handler functions, which require an authenticated user. This annotation should result in a call to a function that checks whether there is an authenticated user. The call must be done before the call to the handler function.

The vibe.d framework provides you with a generic solution. The @before attribute is used to run a function before the annotated handler function is executed. The attribute requires the function to run and a parameter name. The annotated function must have a parameter with this name. The function to run must take a HTTPServerRequest and HTTPServerResponse parameters. The return type must match the type of the parameter.

Here are the changes that you have to apply to the NoteApplication class from the previous section:

1. To store information about the user, you create a new UserData struct. The loggedIn Boolean flag is important, which is only true if the user is successfully authenticated. Other data is the name of the user and unique ID for NoteStore. This struct can be defined outside the NoteApplication class:

   ```
   struct UserData
   {
     bool loggedIn;
     string name;
     string uuid;
   }
   ```

2. In NoteApplication, you can replace the uuid session variable with a new one:

   ```
   private SessionVar!(UserData, "user") user;
   ```

3. The ensureAuth() method checks whether the user is authenticated. This method has the signature required by the @before attribute. As the method is private, you need to mix in some code to allow access:

   ```
   private string ensureAuth(HTTPServerRequest req,
     HTTPServerResponse res)
   {
     if (!user.loggedIn)
       redirect("/");
     return user.name;
   }
   mixin PrivateAccessProxy;
   ```

4. Every method that requires an authenticated user can now be annotated with @before!ensureAuth("_authUser"). This is a lot to type. Therefore, you define a shortcut:

   ```
   private enum auth = before!ensureAuth("_authUser");
   ```

[81]

Easy Forms with the Web Framework

5. The methods can now be annotated with `@auth`. Do not forget to add a `string _authUser` **parameter, too:**

```
void index(string _error = null)
{
  render!("index.dt", _error);
}

@errorDisplay!index
void postLogin(string username, string password)
{
  import std.uuid : randomUUID;

  enforce(username == "yourid" && password == "secret",
    "Invalid username / password");
  UserData d;
  d.loggedIn = true;
  d.name = username;
  d.uuid = randomUUID.toString;
  user = d;
  redirect("/listnotes");
}

@auth
void getListnotes(string _authUser)
{
  auto allnotes = noteStore.getNotes(user.uuid);
  render!("listnotes.dt", allnotes);
}

@method(HTTPMethod.GET)
void logout()
{
  user = UserData.init;
  terminateSession();
  redirect("/");
}

@auth
void getNoteEntry(string _authUser, ValidationErrorData
  _error = ValidationErrorData.init)
{
```

```
      render!("create.dt", _error);
    }

    @auth
    @errorDisplay!getNoteEntry
    void createNewNote(string _authUser, ValidTopic form_topic,
      string form_content)
    {
      Note note;
      note.topic = form_topic;
      note.content = form_content;
      auto allnotes = noteStore.getNotes(user.uuid);
      allnotes ~= note;
      noteStore.setNotes(user.uuid, allnotes);
      redirect("/listnotes");
    }
```

Together with the `index.dt` template in the login form from the previous chapter, this is now a complete web application using input validation and authentication. It can serve as a blueprint for your own web applications.

> There is an @after attribute, too. As the name implies, this attribute is used to annotate a handler method with a function that is run after the handler method. The @after attribute takes no parameter name. Multiple @after annotations are processed in sequence.

This solution does not enable TLS/SSL. All data is transmitted as plain text. In order to make the logging in safe, you have to enable TLS/SSL as described in *Enabling TLS/SSL with your application* section, of *Chapter 3*, *Get Interactive – Forms and Flow Control*.

Localizing the web content

In *Chapter 2*, *Using Templates for Your Web Pages*, you learned how to modify templates to use different languages based on user preferences. With the web framework, the coding is reduced. You need the same `TranslationContext` struct as follows:

```
struct TranslationContext
{
  import std.typetuple : TypeTuple;

  alias languages = TypeTuple!("en_US", "de_DE");
```

```
    mixin translationModule!"example";

    static string determineLanguage(HTTPServerRequest req)
    {
      import std.string : split, replace;

      auto acc_lang = "Accept-Language" in req.headers;
      if (acc_lang)
        return replace(split(*acc_lang, ",")[0], "-", "_");
      return null;
    }
}
```

In order to use this context, you annotate the application class:

```
@translationContext!TranslationContext
class NoteApplication
{ /* ... */ }
```

Then, you can use the `trWeb()` function in your application class to retrieve a translated text. The translation context is also automatically passed to your templates.

Error messages should be treated in a consistent way. An error message that results from a failed validation is not translated. The recommended way is to do the translation in the template file. All error messages that you create in your application are then translated in the template, as well.

Summary

Building on the techniques from the previous chapters, the web framework enables you to code your web application at a more abstract level. The automatic creation of routes and binding of form field values to the parameters of the handler function are the features that boost your productivity. You also learned how to add your own validation functions and display the error message. Security functionality was implemented with the generic `@before` attribute. The web framework also simplifies access to translated text for the localization of your website.

A real web application needs a database for the persistent storage of its data. This is the topic of the next chapter.

5
Accessing a Database

Every web application needs a persistent storage. Depending on your needs, you can choose between different types of databases. The vibe.d framework has built-in support for **MongoDB** and **Redis**, and a native **MySQL** library is available as an external DUB package. The note application is extended in order to use each of these databases.

In this chapter, we will cover the following topics:

- What are the different types of databases and their advantages and disadvantages
- How to connect and use the Redis key-value store
- How to connect and use the MongoDB document database
- How to connect and use the MySQL relational database

Choosing the right database technology

Before extending the note application, let's take a look at the different database technologies available for use.

Relational databases

The predominant type of database is the relational database. The foundation of relational databases is the relational model, a mathematical notation developed in the late sixties by *E. F. Codd*. The basic idea is to define structures and integrity features and manipulations on them. Most relational databases today use **SQL**, the **Structured Query Language**, to implement the relational model. A collection of tables defines the structure of the database. A table is a collection of rows that have the same columns. Each table must have a primary key consisting of one or more columns. The primary key uniquely identifies a row in the table. In order to reference a row in another table, you store the primary key of the referenced row in your table. This is called a foreign key. Integrity demands that the foreign key must exist. Data is retrieved with the `SELECT` command while `INSERT` and `UPDATE` manipulate data. SQL is a standardized language. Once you learn it, you can use it to query databases from different vendors—MySQL being one of them—and we will be using it in this chapter.

A big advantage of relational databases is that they ensure your data integrity. This is always needed if an operation updates tables. Think of balancing your credit card account. You need to reduce your check account and transfer (add) this money to your credit card account. Both operations must take place; otherwise, you or your credit card provider loses money. If you need this property, then you should use a relational database.

The disadvantages are the fixed structure and ensuring integrity limits the distribution and scalability of the database.

A key-value store

With the rise of high-traffic websites, the disadvantages of relational databases become a limiting factor. Consider a web store: customers look for products, which results in many database queries. Eventually, they decide to buy a product and put this product in their basket. This is a database update, but there is no need to check for data integrity because the basket is unique for the customer.

A different requirement is the fast handling of unstructured data. Today, a huge amount of unstructured data is collected, for example, from sensors in a network or log files from applications. Nevertheless, you want to analyze this data in order to gain more insight.

As a consequence, other database types were developed. One approach is to use a key-value store. The key must be unique and must identify a single value. This is like an associative array in D. The power of a key-value store comes from the fact that you can use a variety of data types for the key and value. As the key is really important now, you need to give it some structure. You can use user:yourid as the key to retrieve the password for the user with the yourid name. To store the e-mail address of this user, you can use the user:yourid:email key. With this key structure, you can construct arbitrary collections of the data. A key-value store such as Redis allows you to store struct-like data as the value, which simplifies the design.

The advantage of key-value stores is that they are simple and fast. Most implementations use the main memory to store the data that boost the performance. The persistence of data depends on the database product. Key-value stores can use a cluster to distribute data and replicate data to the other servers. Therefore, they scale very well. If you need the performance and scalability, if the simple key structure fits your application's need and you can forgo data integrity, then you should use a key-value store.

As a disadvantage, key-value stores do not provide transactions. You can do atomic operations, for example, incrementing a value, but this requires special commands in the database. As there is no standardized query language, it may be difficult to use a different key-value store after you have developed your application.

Document databases

Another database type is the document database. In this context, a document is a collection of key-value pairs. The keys define the structure of the document and values are the document content. Unlike a table in a relational database, the documents must not have a fixed structure. Depending on your needs, keys may be optionally present in a document.

A common approach is to present a document in **JavaScript Object Notation (JSON)**. The following is a document representing a note from the note application in JSON:

```
{
  "userid": 123,
  "topic": "A sample topic",
  "content": "Something to remember",
  "creation_time": "2015-05-03 15:18:01"
}
```

The notation is instantly readable. The document has the `"userid"`, `"topic"`, `"content"`, and `"creation_time"` keys. The value is separated by a colon. This document does not contain a reference to an uploaded file. If required, a new `"filename"` key can be added.

Documents are often stored together in groups, which are sometimes called a **collection**. A document database itself is a collection of collections. How to organize the collections depends on your application. The documents in a collection should share some keys; otherwise, they are totally unrelated documents that might be better stored in different collections.

Like a relational database, there are commands to retrieve data and insert, delete, and update data. Unlike a relational database, there is no need to define a scheme. The structure of a single document is defined at the time the application developer inserts the document into the database. The most commonly used document database is MongoDB.

The advantage of document databases is flexibility. As a collection of key-value pairs, a document simplifies the handling of associated data compared to raw key-value stores. The document structure is defined by the application. If there are new requirements during the lifetime of your application, you can simply change the structure of the new documents. The use of documents enables sophisticated query languages, too. There is no need to reorganize the database because of the change possibly causing an outage of your website. Document databases do not support data integrity mechanisms such as a relational database. Therefore, they can easily run on a cluster and replicate the data to other servers, which means that they scale very well. If you need both flexibility and speed and you can forgo data integrity, then you should use a document database.

The flexibility of document databases is also a disadvantage. It is easy to make poor design choices that harm the performance of the database. Document databases are not that different from relational databases, so you have to think about how to structure your data, too. While it is possible to filter documents, complex queries with joins are not supported.

Making a choice

Choosing the right database type is a complex decision. Each database type has advantages and disadvantages over the others. There are no sharp borders as well: databases may implement more than one concept. For example, there are databases that use the key-value concept and document concept together. The best guidance is to list the features that your application requires from a database and base your decision on this list.

Using the Redis key-value store

Redis is the most commonly used key-value store. The vibe.d framework has built-in support for Redis that you can use to provide persistent storage for the note application. For more in-depth information about Redis, take a look at *Instant Redis Persistence* by *Matt Palmer, Packt Publishing*. You can find the book at https://www.packtpub.com/big-data-and-business-intelligence/instant-redis-persistence-instant.

Installing Redis

The source code of Redis is available at http://redis.io/. After downloading and unpacking the source file, you can change over to the source directory and type the following command to build Redis on Unix-like operating systems:

```
$ make
```

Most Linux distributions offer a Redis package that you can use. Let's take a look at how you can install Redis on a few other operating systems:

- On Ubuntu/Debian, type the following to install Redis:
    ```
    $ sudo apt-get install redis-server
    ```
- On Fedora 21 or earlier, you can install Redis with the following:
    ```
    $ sudo yum install redis
    ```
- On Fedora 22, you can type as follows:
    ```
    $ sudo dnf install redis
    ```
- On OS X, the Homebrew package manager can be used to install Redis:
    ```
    $ brew install redis
    ```

There is no official Windows version of Redis, but the Microsoft OpenTech group develops and maintains a Windows 64-bit port.

> You can download an installer at https://github.com/MSOpenTech/redis/releases.

After the installation, you can start the Redis server with sudo /etc/init.d/redis start or sudo /etc/init.d/redis-server start, depending on your distribution. On OS X, you start the Redis server with redis-server /usr/local/etc/redis.conf.

Accessing Redis from the note application

You can use the Redis client, which is a part of vibe.d, to connect to your Redis server. The main class is `RedisClient` from which you get access to the database class, `RedisDatabase`. You only need to add the following code:

```
RedisDatabase db;

shared static this()
{
  auto redis = new RedisClient();
  db = redis.getDatabase(0);
  // Other initialization code
}
```

As the key-value store is a simple data structure, you need to think about the organization of the data. The note application needs access to the user, his/her password, and stored notes of the user. The username is a key. Using the structure from *A key-value store* section, the password is stored as a value of the `user:<username>` key. The SET command sets the value for a key, and the GET command returns the value of a key. Both commands are available as the `set()` and `get()` methods of the `RedisDatabase` class. Authenticating the user is now easy, as follows:

```
bool checkUser(string username, string password)
{
  return db.get("user:" ~ username) == password;
}
```

This method is used instead of the hard-coded username and password:

```
@errorDisplay!index
void postLogin(string username, string password)
{
  enforce(checkUser(username, password),
    "Invalid username / password");
  // Code as before
}
```

With these small changes, the note application asks the Redis database in order to authenticate the user. If you want to try it, you need to populate the database with some user accounts. This can be done with the `redis-cli` command:

```
$ redis-cli
127.0.0.1:6379> SET user:yourid secret
OK
```

```
127.0.0.1:6379> GET user:yourid
"secret"
127.0.0.1:6379> QUIT
```

You can use `redis-cli` to inspect the data written by the application, as well.

Storing the notes requires some more thoughts. A note itself maps to the Redis hash data type. A Redis hash is a map of fields to the values. A note has two fields: topic and content, with the values entered in the user interface. How to construct the key? A list of hashes would be ideal, but this data type is not available with Redis. However, you can emulate it. If each note is identified by a number, then you can store the hash using the `user:<username>:note:<number>` key. The Redis HMSET and HMGET commands set and get multiple fields of a hash. With `redis-cli`, you can enter the following:

```
127.0.0.1:6379> HMSET user:yourid:note:1 topic "First topic" content
"First content"
OK
127.0.0.1:6379> HMGET user:yourid:note:1 topic content
1) "First topic"
2) "First content"
127.0.0.1:6379> QUIT
```

Both commands are available as the `hmset()` and `hmget()` methods of the `RedisDatabase` class. This is a common pattern for all the other Redis commands, too.

For each user, the last used number is stored as the value of the `user:<username>:nextid` key. The INCR command atomically increments the value of a key (if it is a number) and returns the new value. This creates a unique number for each note. Finally, the numbers of the notes are stored in a Redis list. This data type is a linked list with constant access time to the head and tail of the list. The RPUSH command adds an element to the end of the list, LLEN returns the length of the list, and LRANGE returns all the elements between a start and stop index. If a command returns more than one value, the corresponding D method returns a range and implements the functions required for the `foreach` loops. Due to this, the code of the `NoteStore` class is straightforward:

```
    class NoteStore
    {
      Note[] getNotes(string name)
      {
        import std.conv : to;
```

Accessing a Database

```d
    import std.array : array;

    Note[] result = new Note[0];
    auto prefix = "user:" ~ name ~ ":";
    auto noteskey = prefix ~ "notes";
    auto ids = db.lrange!long(noteskey, 0, db.llen(noteskey));
    foreach (id; ids)
    {
      auto data = array(db.hmget(prefix ~ "note:" ~
        to!string(id), "topic", "content"));
      if (!data.empty)
        result ~= Note(id, data[0], data[1]);
    }
    return result;
  }

  void addNote(string name, ref Note note)
  {
    import std.conv : to;

    auto prefix = "user:" ~ name ~ ":";
    note.id = db.incr(prefix ~ "nextid");
    db.hmset(prefix ~ "note:" ~ to!string(note.id), "topic",
      note.topic, "content", note.content);
    db.rpush(prefix ~ "notes", note.id);
  }
}
```

You only need to change the `createNewNote()` and `getListnotes()` methods to use the new interface:

```d
@auth
void getListnotes(string _authUser)
{
  auto allnotes = noteStore.getNotes(user.name);
  render!("listnotes.dt", allnotes);
}

@auth
@errorDisplay!getNoteEntry
void createNewNote(string _authUser, ValidTopic form_topic,
  string form_content)
{
  Note note;
  note.topic = form_topic;
```

[92]

```
    note.content = form_content;
    noteStore.addNote(user.name, note);
    redirect("/listnotes");
}
```

If you want, you can also use Redis as the session store. Just replace `MemorySessionStore` with `RedisSessionStore`. You need to pass the Redis URL and database number to the constructor:

```
shared static this()
{
  import vibe.db.redis.sessionstore;

  // ...
  auto settings = new HTTPServerSettings;
  settings.sessionStore = new RedisSessionStore("127.0.0.1", 0);
  // ...
}
```

This is all that you need to change in order to use Redis as a persistent store for the note application.

Using the MongoDB document database

MongoDB is the most commonly used document database. The vibe.d framework has built-in support for MongoDB, which you can use to provide persistent storage for the note application. For more in-depth information about MongoDB, take a look at *Instant MongoDB* by *Amol Nayak, Packt Publishing*. You can find the book at https://www.packtpub.com/big-data-and-business-intelligence/instant-mongodb-instant.

Installing MongoDB

The website of MongoDB is http://www.mongodb.org/. Here, you can find detailed installation instructions and precompiled binaries for many Linux distributions, OS X, Solaris, and Windows. Building from the source is not as easy as with Redis because MongoDB has external dependencies. For a quick start, you can use the version of your distribution. Now, let's take a look at how we can install MongoDB on different operating systems:

- On Ubuntu/Debian, type the following to install MongoDB:
    ```
    $ sudo apt-get install mongodb-server
    ```

- On Fedora 21 or earlier, you can install MongoDB with the following:

  ```
  $ sudo yum install mongodb
  ```

- On Fedora 22, you type as follows:

  ```
  $ sudo dnf install mongodb
  ```

- On OS X, the `Homebrew` package manager can be used to install MongoDB:

  ```
  $ brew install mongdb
  ```

After the installation, you can start the MongoDB server with `sudo /etc/init.d/mongodb start` or `sudo /etc/init.d/mongodb-server start`, depending on your distribution. On OS X, you can start the MongoDB server with `mongod -config /usr/local/etc/mongod.conf`.

Persisting data with MongoDB

An interface to MongoDB is part of vibe.d. The connection to MongoDB is handled by the `MongoClient` class. Only the URL of the database is required:

```
MongoClient client;

shared static this()
{
  // ...
  client = connectMongoDB("127.0.0.1");
  // ...
}
```

MongoDB stores the data in documents that are organized in collections. The note application uses the `NoteApp` database and stores the user data in the `users` collection and the notes in `notes`. Each document has a unique identifier, `_id`. This identifier can be specified by the application; otherwise, MongoDB generates a unique value. The username can be used as a key. A sample document for the user data is as follows:

```
{ "_id": "yourid", "password": "secret" }
```

You can use the `mongo` shell to populate your MongoDB instance:

```
$ mongo
MongoDB shell version: 2.6.8
connecting to: test
> use NoteApp
Switched to db NoteApp
```

```
> db.NoteApp.users.insert( { "_id": "yourid", "password": "secret" } )
WriteResult({ "nInserted" : 1 })
> exit
bye
```

The D code to authenticate the user is similar. You need to retrieve `MongoCollection` and look up the user:

```
bool checkUser(string username, string password)
{
  MongoCollection users = client.getCollection("NoteApp.users");
  auto result = users.findOne(["_id": username,
    "password": password]);
  return result != Bson(null);
}
```

The collection is prefixed with the database name; otherwise, you have to get a `MongoDatabase` object first. There is no advantage in using the `MongoDatabase` object here, but it is useful in order to become independent of the database name. The `findOne()` method looks up a single object and returns a BSON representation of the object. The `Bson(null)` object is returned if nothing is found and used in the comparison.

The notes belong to a user. This is a one-to-many relationship that can be modeled with an embedded document. A sample note document looks as follows:

```
{
  "user_id": "yourid",
  "notes": [
        { "topic": "Topic 1", "content": "Content 1" },
        { "topic": "Topic 2", "content": "Content 2" }
     ]
}
```

Other designs are possible, for example, storing only the identifier of the notes in the inner document. The choice here emphasizes the document character of the data store.

As the BSON representation is used, you have to convert your D objects to the BSON representation and vice versa. You can use the `serializeBson()` and `deserializeBson()` functions for this purpose. D structs are serialized as associative arrays, which is what you want. If the type can be serialized, then you can use values of the type without converting them first. If the type is not serializable by default, then you can add the `toBson()` or `toJson()` method to provide a custom serialization. A JSON representation is automatically converted to BSON.

Accessing a Database

To use the automatic conversion, you define some structs:

```
struct Note
{
  string topic;
  string content;
}

struct Notes
{
  string user_id;
  Note[] notes;
}
```

The `Notes` struct is the D equivalent of the MongoDB document. With these structs, you can implement the `NoteStore` class:

```
class NoteStore
{
  Note[] getNotes(string name)
  {
    MongoCollection c = client.getCollection("NoteApp.notes");
    auto result = c.findOne(["user_id": name]);
    if (result.isNull)
      return new Note[0];
    Notes notes = deserializeBson!Notes(result);
    return notes.notes;
  }

  void addNote(string name, ref Note note)
  {
    MongoCollection c = client.getCollection("NoteApp.notes");
    c.update(["user_id": name],
      ["$push": ["notes": note]],
      UpdateFlags.Upsert);
  }
}
```

If the `UpdateFlags.Upsert` flag is used with the `update()` method, then the document is created if none exists. This solves the possible race condition that you first check the existence of the document and try to insert or update the document. A second client may have deleted or inserted the same document meanwhile.

[96]

Using the MySQL relational database

MySQL is one of the most popular open source relational databases. There exists an external MySQL client package, which can be used with vibe.d.

Installing MySQL

The central website for MySQL is `http://dev.mysql.com/downloads/`. You can download precompiled binaries for many platforms, including a Windows installer.

All Linux distributions offer a MySQL package, which you can use. Let's take a look at how you can install MySQL on a few other operating systems:

- On Ubuntu/Debian, type the following to install MySQL:

    ```
    $ sudo apt-get install mysql-server
    ```

- On Fedora 21 or earlier, you can install MySQL with the following:

    ```
    $ sudo yum install mysql
    ```

- On Fedora 22, you type as follows:

    ```
    $ sudo dnf install mysql
    ```

- On OS X, the `Homebrew` package manager can be used to install MySQL:

    ```
    $ brew install mysql
    ```

After the installation, you can start the MySQL server with `sudo /etc/init.d/mysql start` or `sudo /etc/init.d/mysql-server start`, depending on your distribution.

Using MySQL with vibe.d

In contrast to Redis and MongoDB, there is no MySQL driver included in vibe.d. The first thing that you have to do is add a new external dependency to the `dub.sdl` file of your project:

```
// ...
dependency "vibe-d" version="~>0.7.23"
dependency "mysql-native" version="~>0.1.2"
// ...
```

There are other D interfaces to MySQL, too. However, this package is tightly integrated with vibe.d so you want to use it. Other packages do not use the I/O model of vibe.d, which requires some additional work. Refer to *Chapter 7, The vibe.d Internals*, for more information.

Accessing a Database

Next, you have to create a SQL schema. A SQL schema is the definition of the tables that hold the data of your application. The authentication data is stored in the `Users` table and the note data is stored in the `Notes` table. Each table has a column `id` that is the primary key. The `Notes` table references the `Users` table with the foreign key in the `userid` column. MySQL has a variety of data types. They always include some length restrictions; therefore, different SQL types are used for string data. You should also create a new database and need to populate the `Users` table. For ease of use, create the `schema.sql` file with the following content:

```sql
CREATE DATABASE NoteApp;

USE NoteApp;

CREATE TABLE Users (
  id MEDIUMINT UNSIGNED NOT NULL AUTO_INCREMENT,
  username CHAR(30) NOT NULL UNIQUE,
  password CHAR(30) NOT NULL,
  PRIMARY KEY (id)
);

CREATE TABLE Notes (
  id MEDIUMINT UNSIGNED NOT NULL AUTO_INCREMENT,
  userid MEDIUMINT UNSIGNED NOT NULL REFERENCES Users(id),
  topic VARCHAR(255) NOT NULL,
  content TEXT NOT NULL,
  PRIMARY KEY (id)
);

INSERT INTO Users (username, password) VALUES ('yourid',
  'secret');
```

Then, you use the `batch` mode to create a database, table, and data:

$ mysql -p < schema.sql

MySQL asks for the password and then creates the objects.

Now you are ready to connect to MySQL. The main class is named `MysqlDB` and is initialized in the `static this()` constructor:

```
MysqlDB db;

shared static this()
{
  // ...
```

[98]

```
    db = new MysqlDB("localhost", "mysql", "password", "NoteApp");
    // ...
}
```

> Note that you must use the database user and password from your installation.

Equipped with a database connection, the authentication data can now be verified. As the schema uses an ID instead of the username as the primary key, you have to return the ID, too:

```
bool checkUser(string username, string password, out uint id)
{
  auto con = db.lockConnection();
  scope(exit) con.close();
  auto cmd = Command(con, "SELECT id FROM Users WHERE username = ? and password = ?");
  cmd.prepare();
  cmd.bindParameter(username, 0);
  cmd.bindParameter(password, 1);
  auto result = cmd.execPreparedResult();
  id = result.length == 1 ? result.front()[0].get!(uint) : 0;
  return result.length == 1;
}
```

In this method, a connection is retrieved from the connection pool, and a scope guard statement is used to clean up the connection on exit. `Command()` holds the SQL statement to be executed. The SQL statement is prepared and then the parameter values are bound. The preparation allows the statement to be executed several times with different parameter values, but it is also a good protection against SQL injection attacks. Therefore, it is used here. If the statement returns a non-empty result, then the returned ID is retrieved from the result set. If you ever worked with JDBC, then this pattern should be familiar to you.

The use of a different primary key requires a change in `UserData`—the ID has to be stored as well:

```
struct UserData
{
  bool loggedIn;
  string name;
  uint userid;
}
```

Accessing a Database

This also requires a change in the `postLogin()` method of the `NoteApplication` class:

```
@errorDisplay!index
void postLogin(string username, string password)
{
  uint userid;
  enforce(checkUser(username, password, userid),
    "Invalid username / password");
  UserData d;
  d.loggedIn = true;
  d.name = username;
  d.userid = userid;
  user = d;
  redirect("/listnotes");
}
```

The `NoteStore` class uses the same access pattern:

```
class NoteStore
{
  Note[] getNotes(uint id)
  {
    Note toNote(Row r)
    {
      Note note;
      r.toStruct(note);
      return note;
    }

    auto con = db.lockConnection();
    scope(exit) con.close();
    auto cmd = Command(con, "SELECT id, topic, content FROM Notes WHERE userid = ?");
    cmd.prepare();
    cmd.bindParameter(id, 0);
    auto result = cmd.execPreparedResult();
    return array(map!(r => toNote(r))(result));
  }

  void addNote(uint id, ref Note note)
  {
    auto con = db.lockConnection();
    scope(exit) con.close();
```

```
      auto cmd = Command(con, "INSERT INTO Notes (userid, topic,
content) VALUES(?, ?, ?)");
      cmd.prepare();
      cmd.bindParameter(id, 0);
      cmd.bindParameter(note.topic, 1);
      cmd.bindParameter(note.content, 2);
      ulong changed;
      cmd.execPrepared(changed);
   }
}
```

The most interesting part is the handling of `ResultSet`. `ResultSet` is a range of the `Row` objects. This range is mapped to a range of the `Note` objects using the map algorithm and a lambda function. Then, this range is turned into a `Note[]` array with the help of the `array()` function.

The `getListnotes()` and `createNewNote()` methods must be changed as well, because of the changed primary key:

```
@auth
void getListnotes(string _authUser)
{
  auto allnotes = noteStore.getNotes(user.userid);
  render!("listnotes.dt", allnotes);
}

@auth
@errorDisplay!getNoteEntry
void createNewNote(string _authUser, ValidTopic form_topic,
  string form_content)
{
  Note note;
  note.topic = form_topic;
  note.content = form_content;
  noteStore.addNote(user.userid, note);
  redirect("/listnotes");
}
```

MySQL requires the same coding effort as Redis or MongoDB. However, there is one difference: only SQL requires you to specify the length of the data fields. The checks for the lengths are omitted here, but can be easily added as in the previous chapter.

Summary

In this chapter, you learned about different database types and their advantages and disadvantages. At least three different databases are supported by vibe.d, each of a different type. We used all the databases to implement the persistent storage for the note application, which allows us to compare the coding style of each database.

With persistent stored data, our application is now ready to either offer services to other clients or consume services from them. Providing and consuming REST services is the topic of the next chapter.

6
Using the REST Interface

Applications are usually built using components that can be distributed on the network. The protocol that is used to communicate with remote components should be fast but simple to use. **Representational State Transfer** (**REST**) is a software architecture style based on the principles of HTTP—the protocol of the **World Wide Web** (**WWW**). Combined with simple data representation, REST is a popular way to access remote components or services.

In this chapter, we will cover the following topics:

- What is REST and how it uses JSON
- How to expose an interface via REST
- How to access a component remotely via REST
- How to tailor the URL path and parameter passing

Defining the principles of the World Wide Web

As soon as computers were networked, people created binary protocols to execute code on a remote computer. The disadvantage of these **Remote Procedure Call** (**RPC**) protocols is the system dependency. Due to the binary nature, it is not easy to get a remote procedure call right: the size of data types, endianness, and alignment may be different on the target machine. With the success of the WWW, the idea of services appeared. A service provides some functionality, for example, retrieving the stock price at NASDAQ in real time. **Simple Object Access Protocol** (**SOAP**) was created. SOAP is based on XML and, therefore, enables structured data exchange in heterogeneous networks. **Web Service Description Language** (**WSDL**) was created to describe the services, again in XML.

Using the REST Interface

The combination of SOAP and WSDL is used to look up services and generate language bindings for them. This works very well, but there are drawbacks. SOAP is designed to be independent of the transport layer. HTTP is often used but other protocols, including e-mail, are possible. Due to this, SOAP contains certain features that are also available with HTTP. Instead of encrypting the SOAP message, you can use an encrypted HTTP connection. Another drawback is that you lose flexibility because most tools generate code from the service description and cannot handle additions to the service description without rerunning the code generator.

Another approach is to utilize the success factors of the WWW. **Uniform Resource Locator (URL)** already describes a resource in a unique way. The HTTP method is an action on this resource: GET can be interpreted to retrieve data while POST creates some data, PUT updates the data, and DELETE deletes it. Combine this with a data representation such as JSON or XML and you have a simple service defined. REST is a software architecture based on this approach. Due to this, you will not find a REST standard. A software architecture is called REST if it adheres to the following constraints:

- There is a uniform interface between the client and server. This can be the HTTP communication described previously
- The communication is stateless
- The client can cache responses
- The system is layered, for example, a client does not know if it is directly connected to a server or through a proxy

If a system fulfils these constraints, it is called RESTful.

From the point of view of the system architecture, it is not an easy decision between SOAP/WSDL and REST because of the many different details. However, vibe.d currently supports REST only, which has been used in this chapter.

Serializing D to JSON and back

With the RESTful approach, the client and server exchange messages using the HTTP protocol. Of the many possible data formats, **JavaScript Object Notation (JSON)** is used. Originally, JSON was based on a subset of JavaScript. It has basic data types for numbers, strings, and Booleans. Like JavaScript, it uses two different structures to create complex data:

- A collection of key/value pairs called an **object** in JSON. This is like an associative array in D and can be used to represent objects, maps, and so on. The key/value pairs are surrounded by { and }.

- An ordered list of values called an **array** in JSON. The values are surrounded by [and].

The format is written in JavaScript. Once properly formatted, this is easily readable. A list of notes could look as follows:

```
[
    { "id":1, "topic":"Topic 1", "content":"Content 1" },
    { "id":2, "topic":"Topic 2", "content":"Content 2" }
]
```

A single note is the key/value collection in { }. The list consists of the enumerated notes in [ ]. It is possible to construct arbitrarily complex data representations with this approach.

JSON is human readable. This is a big advantage while debugging, but the text representation is less compact and always requires the receiver to parse the message. A binary representation called **Binary JSON (BSON)** was developed to address these issues. BSON is supported by vibe.d as well. However, it is not used for REST but for the MongoDB protocol.

D types are serialized to JSON in a straightforward way. D basic types are mapped to the corresponding basic JSON type. D arrays are mapped to JSON arrays and D `struct` types, `class` types, and associative arrays are mapped to JSON objects.

A `Json` struct (declared in the `vibe.data.json` module) is used to hold a single JSON value. In order to serialize a note, you can write the following:

```
Note note = { 1, "Topic 1", "Content 1" };
auto json = serializeToJson(note);
auto jsonString = json.toString();
```

The `serializeToJsonString()` function creates a string in one call. The `serializeToPrettyJson()` function creates a JSON string with white space and new lines are added for better readability.

To deserialize a JSON string, you can type the following:

```
auto json =
    parseJsonString(`{"id":1,"topic":"t1","content":"c1"}`);
auto note = deserializeJson!Note(json);
```

Using the REST Interface

You can change the serialization, too. You need to implement only one of the following function pairs in `struct` or `class`. The first one is as follows:

```
Json toJson() const;
static T fromJson(Json src);
```

Here is the second one:

```
string toString() const;
static T fromString(string src);
```

One use case is if you want to map an enumeration value to the string literal instead of the integer value. Let's suppose that you have the following enumeration:

```
enum Color { Red, Green, Blue }
```

The standard serialization maps `Color.Red` to 0, `Color.Green` to 1, and `Color.Blue` to 2. The following code maps the values to `Red`, `Green`, and `Blue` instead:

```
struct ColorHolder
{
  import std.conv: to;
  Color color;

  const Json toJson()
  {
    return Json(color.to!string());
  }

  static ColorHolder fromJson(Json src)
  {
    return ColorHolder(src.deserializeJson!string().to!Color());
  }
}
```

Creating and using a REST service

The `NoteStore` class is used to persist and retrieve notes. Because other applications may require this functionality, too, you want to provide it as a service. Starting with the implementation based on Redis from *Chapter 5, Accessing a Database*, you can extract the following interface and save it is as `notestore.d`:

```
module notestore;

struct Note
{
```

```
    long id;
    string topic;
    string content;
}

interface NoteStore
{
    Note[] getNotes(string name);
    long addNote(string name, Note note);
}
```

The only change here is that `addNote()` cannot have a `ref Note` parameter. The reason is that the caller of the method lives in a different process that is possible on a different computer. Therefore, the Note struct of the caller cannot be changed.

The server and client both require this interface. You use a separate module for it.

Providing a service

Let's create the server side. The main difference from the previous implementations is that the implementation of the `NoteStore` interface is registered as a REST service via a call to the `registerRestInterface()` method:

1. Create a new project with `dub`:

   ```
   $ dub init noteapp_server --type=vibe.d
   ```

2. Copy the `notestore.d` module we just saved in the previous section to the `source` folder.

3. Implement the functionality in the `app.d` module in the `source` folder. The implementation is based on the Redis version from *Chapter 5, Accessing a Database*:

   ```
   import vibe.d;
   import notestore;
   import std.conv : to;
   import std.format : format;

   shared static this()
   {
       auto redis = new RedisClient();

       auto noteStore = new
         NoteStoreImplementation(redis.getDatabase(0));

       auto router = new URLRouter;
   ```

```
    router.registerRestInterface(noteStore);

    auto settings = new HTTPServerSettings;
    settings.port = 8081;
    settings.bindAddresses = ["::1", "127.0.0.1"];
    listenHTTP(settings, router);

    logInfo("Please open http://127.0.0.1:8081/ in your
      browser.");
}

class NoteStoreImplementation : NoteStore
{
  RedisDatabase db;

  this(RedisDatabase db)
  {
    this.db = db;
  }

  Note[] getNotes(string name)
  {
    import std.array : array;

    Note[] result = new Note[0];
    auto prefix = format("user:%s", name);
    auto noteskey = format("%s:notes", prefix);
    auto ids = db.lrange!long(noteskey, 0,
      db.llen(noteskey));
    foreach (id; ids)
    {
      auto key = format("%s:note:%d", prefix, id);
      auto data = array(db.hmget(key, "topic",
        "content"));
      if (!data.empty)
        result ~= Note(id, data[0], data[1]);
    }
    return result;
  }

  long addNote(string name, Note note)
  {
    auto prefix = format("user:%s", name);
    note.id = db.incr(format("%s:nextid", prefix));
```

```
        db.hmset(format("%s:note:%d", prefix, note.id),
          "topic", note.topic, "content", note.content);
        db.rpush(format("%s:notes", prefix), note.id);
        return note.id;
    }
}
```

With the call to `registerRestInterface()`, vibe.d adds routes that correspond with the names of the methods in the `NoteStore` interface. It uses the same algorithm as the web framework described in *Chapter 4, Easy Forms with the Web Framework*. The details of the path generation are explained here.

Start your Redis database, run this application, and open `http://127.0.0.1:8081/notes?name=yourid` in your browser. If the database still has the content from the previous chapters, then you can see a JSON representation of it in your browser.

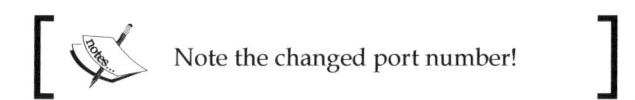

> Note the changed port number!

Using a service

Using the previously created service is simple, as follows:

1. Create a copy of the note application based on the Redis database from *Chapter 5, Accessing a Database*.
2. Copy the `notestore.d` module we just saved in the previous section to the `source` folder.
3. In the `app.d` module, you need to make the following changes:
    - Add an `import notestore;` statement at the top of the file.
    - Delete the `NoteStore` class and the `Note` struct because they are now imported.
    - Delete the `noteStore` variable and the `static this()` constructor that initializes this variable.
    - Add the following code to use a `NoteStore` service via REST:
      ```
      private __gshared RestInterfaceClient!NoteStore noteStore;

      shared static this()
      {
        noteStore = new RestInterfaceClient!NoteStore(
          "http://127.0.0.1:8081/");
      }
      ```

Instantiating the `RestInterfaceClient` class generates a proxy class that forwards all the method calls to the remote service at `http://127.0.0.1:8081`.

To test your new application, you need to start the Redis database, server application from the previous section, and this client application.

Tailoring the generated REST API

REST is really a tool for service integration. To match the requirements of an existing service, you need control of several parameters such as the path, HTTP method, or header parameters.

Changing the generated path

As in the case of a web application, the URL path and HTTP method is derived from the function to be called.

A `@property` method uses the HTTP GET method to read the property and PUT to write the property. The HTTP method of all the other methods is derived from the prefix of the method name:

Prefix	HTTP method
get	GET
query	GET
set	PUT
put	PUT
update	PATCH
patch	PATCH
add	POST
create	POST
post	POST
remove	DELETE
erase	DELETE
delete	DELETE

The default HTTP POST method is used if the method is neither an `@property` method nor a method that can be derived from the preceding table. You can set the HTTP method with the `@method` annotation:

```
@method(HTTPMethod.GET)
Note retrieveNote();
```

This overrides the default POST method with GET.

The URL path is created from the method name. First, the prefix, according to the preceding table, is removed. Then, the remaining string is mapped using the chosen naming scheme. The default naming scheme is MethodStyle.lowerUnderscored: an underscore is inserted in front of every upper character and then all the characters are made lowercase. For example, the getAllMyData() method name is mapped to all_my_data. The naming scheme is an optional parameter of the registerRestInterface() method. Just pass a different value if you want a different naming scheme. The following are the possible values:

Name	Example
camelCase	allMyData
lowercase	allmydata
lowerUnderscored	all_my_data
PascalCase	AllMyData
unaltered	getAllMyData
uppercase	ALLMYDATA
upperUnderscored	ALL_MY_DATA

You can override the name with the @path attribute. It is also possible to specify a relative path with @path:

```
@path("note/all")
Note[] getAllNotes();
```

The getAllNotes() method is now called with GET /note/all instead of GET /all_notes.

A common URL prefix can be set with the @path annotation as follows:

```
@path("notestore")
interface NoteStore
{
   long addNote(string name, Note note);
}
```

The addNote() method is now called with POST /notestore/note instead of POST /note.

As an alternative, you can use @rootPathFromName. Then the URL prefix is derived from the interface name. This is a shorthand for @path("").

If the first parameter of a method is named `id`, then this parameter is mapped to the `void putData(string id, string data);` path using the `/:id/data` path. This is really a legacy mechanism but you must be aware of it in order to avoid surprises. There is also a more generalized approach. If a parameter name starts with an underscore, then this parameter is not serialized. Instead, it is available as a placeholder and can be used for path generation. Let's take a look at the following declaration:

```
@method(HTPPMethod.GET)
@path(":name")
void existsDatabase(string _name)
```

This results in `GET /notestore` if the method is called with `_name` set to `notestore`.

This flexibility to change the generated path is useful if you want to access an existing service.

Passing parameters

If a method of a REST interface is called, the parameters are passed as a query string if the HTTP `GET` or `HEAD` methods are used. Otherwise, they are serialized to JSON and transmitted in the request body. This behavior can be changed with the following annotations:

- With `@headerParam`, the parameter is passed in the HTTP header. This can be used to add new elements to the header, for example, an `If-Match` header:

  ```
  @headerParam("rev", "If-Match")
  void postData(string rev, string data)
  ```

- With `@queryParam`, the parameter is passed in the query string. In the example, the value of the `query` parameter is appended as `?param=<value of parameter query>` to the request URL:

  ```
  @queryParam("query", "param")
  void postData(string query, string otherdata)
  ```

- With `@bodyParam`, the parameter becomes part of the JSON object transmitted in the request body. A limitation here is that serialization in the JSON object is not customizable. This can be used to create request bodies if the HTTP `GET` method is used:

  ```
  @bodyParam("data", "content")
  void getData(string data)
  ```

Accessing CouchDB

The `NoteStore` service and `NoteApp` client from the previous sections were written in D. Therefore, there was no problem in using the service. However, the main idea of REST is to be independent of the service implementation. This is best shown by using a different service.

CouchDB is another document-based database. It is written in the **Erlang** programming language and offers a REST interface that you can use to implement `NoteStore`.

Installing CouchDB

The website of CouchDB is `http://couchdb.apache.org/`. Here, you can find detailed installation instructions and precompiled binaries for OS X and Windows. Building from the source requires the Erlang programming language. For a quick start, you can use the version of your distribution:

- On Ubuntu/Debian, type the following to install CouchDB:
  ```
  $ sudo apt-get install couchdb
  ```
- On Fedora 21 or earlier, you can install CouchDB with the following:
  ```
  $ sudo yum install couchdb
  ```
- On Fedora 22, you type as follows:
  ```
  $ sudo dnf install couchdb
  ```
- On OS X, the `Homebrew` package manager can be used to install CouchDB:
  ```
  $ brew install couchdb
  ```

After the installation, you can start the CouchDB server with `sudo /etc/init.d/couchdb`. On OS X, you can start the CouchDB server with `launchctl load /usr/local/Cellar/couchdb/1.6.1_3/homebrew.mxcl.couchdb.plist`.

Testing the REST interface

CouchDB listens on port 5984 for the incoming HTTP requests.

> The complete API is documented online at `http://docs.couchdb.org/en/1.6.1/api/index.html`.

Using the REST Interface

The vibe.d framework includes an HTTP client class that is used by the generated REST client. You need to make the decision if you want to use `RestInterfaceClient` or if you have to create your own access class using the HTTP client. If you scan through the online documentation of CouchDB, then you can note the following deficiencies of `RestInterfaceClient`:

- You have no access to the HTTP status code for successful requests. If the request fails, then the HTTP status code is available in `RestException` thrown by `RestInterfaceClient`.
- `RestInterfaceClient` requires a non-empty response body. However, CouchDB provides you with some check APIs that only return an HTTP status code and empty body.

For a full-features interface to CouchDB, these restrictions may not be acceptable. However, to implement `NoteStore`, only some API calls are required. The decision is to go with `RestInterfaceClient` because it reduces the effort to implement the required functionality.

To develop the interface class, it is helpful to use a small test application. Create a new project with the following:

```
$ dub init couchdb --type=vibe.d
```

Then replace `VibeDefaultMain` with `VibeCustomMain` in the `dub.sdl` file. Now you can use a `main()` method.

Another tool that you can use is the logging infrastructure. Every example application outputs a short message using `logInfo()`. The framework itself uses different logging levels to output diagnostic messages. The default is to output only informational messages, warnings, and errors. This can be changed with the `setLogLevel()` method. Setting the level to `LogLevel.verbose2` outputs the request URLs and the request and response bodies.

Let's try to get some information about CouchDB and create a database. A GET request to the base URL returns information about CouchDB. A GET request with a single path element returns information about the database with the name of the path element or status code 404 if the database does not exist. A PUT request with a single path element creates the database or returns a status code 412 if the database already exists.

> Remember that `RestInterfaceClient` throws `RestException` if the HTTP status code does not indicate a successful execution!

With this API information, you can write your first CouchDB client that you can put in the app.d module of the previously created project:

```d
import vibe.d;

interface CouchDB
{
  Json get();

  @method(HTTPMethod.GET)
  @path(":db")
  Json existsDB(string _db);

  @method(HTTPMethod.PUT)
  @path(":db")
  Json createDB(string _db);
}

void main()
{
  // Uncomment to see the requests
  // setLogLevel(LogLevel.verbose2);
  auto couchdb = new
    RestInterfaceClient!CouchDB("http://127.0.0.1:5984/");

  auto ver = couchdb.get();
  logInfo("CouchDB: %s", ver["couchdb"].to!string);
  logInfo("Version: %s", ver["version"].to!string);
  logInfo("Vendor-Version: %s",
    ver["vendor"]["version"].to!string);
  logInfo("Vendor-Name: %s", ver["vendor"]["name"].to!string);
  logInfo("UUID: %s", ver["uuid"].to!string);

  try
  {
    couchdb.existsDB("notestore");
    logInfo("Database exists");
  }
  catch (RestException e)
  {
    logInfo("Database does not exist (HTTP status code %d)",
      e.status);

    couchdb.createDB("notestore");
  }
}
```

The `CouchDB` interface uses the `Json` structure as the return type. It contains the parsed JSON string. You need to use this if the structure of the JSON string changes dynamically and cannot be mapped to a D structure. In this case, it is simply saved to define a D structure for the deserialization.

The `get()` method does not have a good name; `getWelcome()` would be better. The point here is that according to the rules, the `get` prefix is stripped from the method name, which results in an empty name. This results in a GET request to the base URL. There is no other way to specify this. The `@path("/")` or `@path("")` annotations are not allowed.

Implementing the NoteStore service

Encouraged by the success of the sample application, you can now implement the `NoteStore` class with CouchDB as a persistent store. The CouchDB API for documents is very similar to that for the CouchDB database. The first path element is again the database and the second path element is the document name.

As a special feature, CouchDB uses optimistic locking. Each document has a revision. If you want to update a document, you have to specify the revision of the document as well. If the current revision of the document in the database does not match the revision that you have provided, then somebody else has modified the document, your update conflicts with the current state of the database and this is indicated by the HTTP status code 409 (`HTTPStatus.conflict`). In this case, you have to retry your update. As this is a potentially infinite process, you have to use a loop.

Together, this leads to the following implementation of the `NoteStore` class. At first, you import the required modules and define the `CouchDB` interface with the needed database methods. This interface makes use of many of the annotations introduced earlier in this chapter:

```
import vibe.d;
import notestore;

interface CouchDB
{
  Json get();

  @method(HTTPMethod.GET)
  @path(":name")
  Json existsDB(string _name);

  @method(HTTPMethod.PUT)
  @path(":db")
```

```
    Json createDB(string _db);

    @method(HTTPMethod.PUT)
    @path(":db/:docid")
    @headerParam("rev", "If-Match")
    void updateDoc(string _db, string _docid, string rev, Json doc);

    @method(HTTPMethod.PUT)
    @path(":db/:docid")
    void createDoc(string _db, string _docid, Json doc);

    @method(HTTPMethod.DELETE)
    @path(":db/:docid")
    @headerParam("rev", "If-Match")
    void deleteDoc(string _db, string _docid, string rev);

    @method(HTTPMethod.GET)
    @path(":db/:docid")
    Json retrieveDoc(string _db, string _docid, bool latest =
      false);
}
```

Next, you define the `static this()` constructor. A REST client for `CouchDB` is instantiated. This `CouchDB` instance is used by the `NoteStore` implementation. The `NoteStore` instance is then exported as a REST interface:

```
shared static this()
{
  auto couchdb = new
    RestInterfaceClient!CouchDB("http://127.0.0.1:5984/");

  auto noteStore = new NoteStoreImplementation(couchdb);

  auto router = new URLRouter;
  router.registerRestInterface(noteStore);

  auto settings = new HTTPServerSettings;
  settings.port = 8081;
  settings.bindAddresses = ["::1", "127.0.0.1"];
  listenHTTP(settings, router);

  logInfo("Please open http://127.0.0.1:8081/ in your browser.");
}
```

Using the REST Interface

Finally, you implement the `NoteStore` interface using `CouchDB`. The implementation is straightforward except for one detail. `CouchDB` uses optimistic locking. If you try to update a document and the version of the document does not match, then an exception is thrown. This happens if someone else has already updated the document. The solution is to retry the operation with the updated document. Another detail to notice is that the client is not responsible for providing the `id` of a new `Note`. Therefore, it is necessary to figure out which `id` to use:

```
class NoteStoreImplementation : NoteStore
{
  RestInterfaceClient!CouchDB db;

  this(RestInterfaceClient!CouchDB db)
  {
    this.db = db;
  }

  Note[] getNotes(string name)
  {
    try
    {
      auto doc = db.retrieveDoc("notestore", name, true);
      return deserializeJson!(Note[])(doc["doc"]);
    }
    catch (RestException e)
    {
      if (e.status == HTTPStatus.notFound)
        return new Note[0];
      throw e;
    }
  }

  long addNote(string name, Note note)
  {
    while (true)
    {
      try
      {
        try
        {
          auto doc = db.retrieveDoc("notestore", name, true);
          Note[] notes;
          if (doc["doc"].type() != Json.Type.undefined)
            notes = deserializeJson!(Note[])(doc["doc"]);
```

```
              else
                notes = new Note[0];
              long id = 0;
              foreach (n; notes) id = max(id, n.id);

              note.id = id+1;
              notes ~= note;

              db.updateDoc("notestore", name,
                doc["_rev"].to!string,
                serializeToJson(notes));
            }
            catch (RestException e)
            {
              if (e.status != HTTPStatus.notFound) throw e;
              Note[] notes = new Note[1];
              note.id = 1;
              notes[0] = note;

              db.createDoc("notestore", name,
                serializeToJson(notes));
            }
            return note.id;
          }
          catch (RestException e)
          {
            if (e.status != HTTPStatus.conflict) throw e;
          }
        }
      }
    }
```

This implementation can be used as a replacement for the `NoteStore` service based on the Redis database from the *Creating and using a REST service* section. The structure of the application that you have now created is as follows:

- The web application listens on port 8080 for requests from web browsers. It uses the Redis database to store usernames and their passwords.
- The Redis database uses a proprietary protocol and listens on port 6379.
- The `NoteStore` service provides persistence for notes. It provides a REST interface and listens on port 8081 for the incoming requests.
- Finally, a note is stored in CouchDB. This is again an application that provides a REST interface and listens on port 5984.

All these servers can be installed on different nodes on the Internet: this is a distributed application! This application adheres to the REST principle mentioned in the *Defining the principles of the World Wide Web* section, and it is a RESTful application!

Summary

In this chapter, RESTful systems were introduced. The HTTP protocol is used for lightweight remote access using JSON objects as the data format. You learned how to create and consume a REST service with vibe.d. You also learned how to tailor the REST request, which is very useful if you have to match an existing interface. For testing purposes, you created an application that used its own `main()` method.

The difference between the `main()` method provided by vibe.d and your own `main()` method and the other internals of vibe.d are the topics of the next chapter.

The vibe.d Internals

The vibe.d framework uses asynchronous I/Os and fibers under the hood. The framework shields the developer from the complexity introduced by these techniques. This is called the **fiber-based pseudo-blocking programming model**. With the knowledge about the internals of vibe.d, you will be able to change the existing components to take advantage of vibe.d.

In this chapter, we will cover the following topics:

- The advantages of the fiber-based pseudo-blocking programming model
- A comparison of fiber-based and thread-based models
- The steps needed to port an existing component to vibe.d

The programming model of vibe.d

The key to the scalability of vibe.d is the use of asynchronous I/O in combination with fibers.

What is a fiber?

Modern operating systems implement preemptive multitasking. A thread runs until its time slice is exhausted or it must wait for an I/O operation. Then the kernel chooses a different thread to run. Ultimately, the scheduler in the kernel controls the threads.

The vibe.d Internals

In contrast, fibers are a form of cooperative multitasking. As the name implies, cooperative multitasking requires some help from the user functions. A function runs up to a point where the developer decides would be a good place to run another task. Usually, a library function named `yield()` is called, which continues the execution of another function. This is best shown with an example. Here is a simplified version of the classic producer-consumer pattern:

```d
import std.stdio;
import std.math;
import core.thread;

private int goods;
private bool exit;

void producerFiber()
{
  foreach (i; 0..3)
  {
    goods = i^^2;
    writeln("Produced %s", goods);
    Thread.sleep(500.msecs);
    Fiber.yield();
  }
}

void consumerFiber()
{
  while (!exit)
  {
    /* do something */
    writeln("Consumed %s", goods);
    Thread.sleep(500.msecs);
    Fiber.yield();
  }
}

void main()
{
  auto producer = new Fiber(&producerFiber);
  auto consumer = new Fiber(&consumerFiber);
  while (producer.state != Fiber.State.TERM)
  {
    producer.call();
    exit = producer.state == Fiber.State.TERM;
```

```
        consumer.call();
    }
}
```

The `main()` function acts like a scheduler. First, the fibers for the producer and consumer are initialized. Then control is transferred to the producer. The producer does some work, simulated by filling an array with integer values. After some items are produced, a consumer can make use of them; `Fiber.yield()` is called to transfer control to the `main()` function.

> Note that the loop in the producer is not yet finished; the function is still active.

Now the consumer is called. The consumer reads the produced items, does some work, and transfers the control back. Now the loops in the producer and consumer are not finished—both functions are running side by side. Therefore, fibers are also called **coroutines**.

You should take some time to make sure that you really understand fibers and the implications of using them. The example is very simple but illustrates the advantages. Fibers are implemented in the user mode and do not require a switch to the kernel mode. Therefore, they have less overhead. Explicit synchronization is not required; the shared `goods` variable can be accessed by both fibers without protection. The obvious disadvantage of fibers is that the developer must call `Fiber.yield()` at regular intervals. Otherwise, there is no progress in the other fibers.

It is possible to combine pre-emptive multitasking and fibers. A common approach is that each thread in the application uses a set of fibers to perform the work. Windows 7 calls this model **user mode threads**. The D implementation allows the migration of fibers between threads but this is not supported by all the compilers. Operating system constraints must also be considered. For example, an operating system may enforce that a mutex must be unlocked by the thread who acquired the lock. This is problematic if you acquire the lock in a fiber and then the fiber is migrated to another thread.

Benefits of asynchronous I/O

Think of an HTTP server that has to handle several requests, possibly at the same time. In order to read data from the socket, you call the `read()` function of the C library. Without special preparation, this call is returned only after all the requested bytes are copied to the provided buffer. This is what most developers expect and there is nothing wrong with it. However, instead of waiting for the completion of the `read()` function, the server could work on another request. How to implement this?

A common solution is to use multiple threads. For each incoming request, a thread is used. This thread handles the request and creates the response. After this, the thread can be used to process another request.

The drawback of this solution is that it does not scale very well. A thread is usually a kernel object: it is managed by the kernel and requires some space in the kernel. Handling ten thousands of requests means managing tens of thousands of threads, all competing for the same CPU cycles. This is not as efficient as using only a handful of threads.

A better solution is to use asynchronous I/O. This requires putting the socket in the non-blocking mode. A call to `read()` then returns immediately, either with the data or with the hint that the data will be available later. The manner in which your application is informed about available data depends on the operating system. By default, vibe.d uses the `libevent` library for notification. This library creates an event abstraction using the operating system mechanisms. The basic idea is that the availability of the data, timeout, new file in a directory, or many other things are events that are processed in an event loop. The vibe.d framework provides you with a complete set of functions (TCP/UDP connections, file I/O, timers, and so on) to work with the event library. On the surface, these functions work like the blocking version of the same function. Under the hood, they use an event loop and fibers.

Combining threads, fibers, and asynchronous I/O

In the case of the HTTP server, the normal control flow is to read the request, process the request, and, finally, write the response. Using asynchronous I/O, other work can be performed while waiting for the `read()` and `write()` operations. If the developer has to code it manually, then the normal control flow becomes complex and error-prone. Instead, vibe.d handles this transparently: if the developer invokes `read()` or `write()`, then vibe.d automatically transfers control to the event loop. As long as the operation is not yet complete, other fibers may run. Eventually, the operation is done and control is transferred back. For the developer, the operation seems to be blocking. Even if an error occurs, then an exception is raised. This approach is called the fiber-based pseudo-blocking programming model.

By default, vibe.d uses only a single thread. Modern CPUs have multiple cores. Using only one underutilizes the CPU. The requests can be automatically distributed among a thread pool. All you have to do is set `HTTPServerOption.distribute` in the `HTTPServerSettings.options` field during initialization:

```
shared static this()
{
```

```
    /* ... */
    auto settings = new HTTPServerSettings;
    settings.options = HTTPServerOption.distribute;
    /* ... */
}
```

> Be aware that as soon as you switch from a single thread to multiple threads, you need to think about race conditions when accessing and updating data structures.

Using threads is only one option to scale your application. Another option is to run multiple instances of your application. One advantage of this model is a certain degree of fault tolerance: the crash of one instance does not affect the other running instances. This approach requires the use of a load balancer. The `vibedist` project provides you with a load balancer ready to use with vibe.d. See *Chapter 9, Power Your Application with vibe.d Extensions*, on how to install and use additional projects.

Coding your own main function

Almost all sample applications used a `static this()` constructor for initialization. The `main()` function provided by vibe.d is used if the `VibeDefaultMain` version is set in the `dub.sdl` file. Basically, the `main()` function contains the following code:

```
int main()
{
   import vibe.core.args : finalizeCommandLineOptions;
   import vibe.core.core : runEventLoop, lowerPrivileges;

   if (!finalizeCommandLineOptions()) return 0;
   lowerPrivileges();
   return runEventLoop();
}
```

First, the parsing of the command-line options is finalized. Then privileges are dropped if requested and the event loop is started.

The vibe.d Internals

Your code can retrieve the value of options, too. The `readOption()` and `readRequiredOption()` functions return the value of an option. These functions differ in that the latter function enforces that the option exists, throwing an exception if it does not exist. Options can be specified on the command line and also in the `vibe.conf` configuration file. On a Unix system, the file is searched in the home folder of the user and the `/etc/vibe/` global folder. On Windows, the file is searched in the user profile folder because there is no global folder for configuration files.

Some applications require super user rights, usually during initialization. An example is listening on a TCP/IP port with a number lower than 1024. It is a good practice to drop these extra privileges after initialization. Otherwise, you might introduce a security flaw. The reality is that each piece of software contains programming errors that enable an attacker to run his code in the application. If the hijacked application is running with extended privileges, then the attacker can use them for his purposes too. The user can be specified with the `--user` or `--uid` command-line option and the group with `--group` or `--gid`. Like any other option, this can also be specified in the `vibe.conf` file.

With the `VibeDebugCatchAll` version defined, the event loop is placed in a `try ... catch` block. This is useful for the debugging because the full exception information is logged.

> Note that this should not be used for production: only serious error conditions such as out of memory should occur here. In this case, it is dangerous to execute additional diagnostic functions as it is unclear how corrupted the application already is.

If you want to use your own `main()` function, then you have to specify the `VibeCustomMain` version instead of `VibeDefaultMain` in the `dub.sdl` file:

```
versions "VibeCustomMain"
```

> Starting with vibe.d 0.7.26, `VibeCustomMain` is the default.

If you initialize other parts of your application in a `static this()` constructor, then you should not forget to run the event loop. Otherwise, your application will not work.

[126]

You can create applications without an event loop, too. A typical example is a command-line tool such as **Wget**. Downloading a file from the network is a one-liner without an explicit event loop:

```
import vibe.d;

void main()
{
  download("http://packtpub.com/", "index.html");
}
```

As a rule of thumb, you do not need an event loop if your application deals with only a single connection in a sequential manner.

Performing background work

Some tasks are better performed in the background than in a request-response cycle. Depending on the type of work, you can use a fiber-based task or thread.

Running a fiber-based task

A function or method that returns `void` can be started as a fiber-based task with the `runTask()` function. The parameters are the delegates (use `std.functional.toDelegate()` if you have a function) and possible parameters.

> Do not forget to be cooperative in your fiber: call a pseudo-blocking function or `yield()` from time to time.

You can use such a background task to collect data about the server. With the next example, you can read the `/proc/loadavg` file on Linux and collect the data of the last 10 minutes. On a request from a client, you send some JavaScript code to paint the graph of the values. The code uses the `sleep()` function that triggers the switch to the event loop. Collecting the data is very lightweight but the timing is very inaccurate. You should not expect to see a perfect timeline of the load. Here is how to do it:

1. Create a new project with `dub`:

    ```
    $ dub init loadavg --type=vibe.d
    ```

2. Change the app.d module in the source folder to contain the code that collects the loaded data. The only complication is that the kernel does not return the real size of the /proc/loadavg file. Due to this, the standard read() method fails. The work around here is to read the file byte by byte:

```d
import vibe.d;

private string readProcLoadavg()
{
  char[64] buffer;

  auto file = openFile("/proc/loadavg");
  scope(exit) file.close();
  int i = 0;
  while (i < buffer.length)
  {
    file.read(*cast(ubyte[1]*) &buffer[i]);
    if (buffer[i] == '\n') break;
    ++i;
  }
  return buffer[0 .. i].idup;
}

struct Load
{
  float last1, last5, last15;
  int active, total, lastPid;
}

Load[1200] loadData;
int next;

private void collectLoadavg()
{
  import std.format;

  while (true)
  {
    auto res = readProcLoadavg();
    auto p = &loadData[next];
    formattedRead(res, "%f %f %f %d/%d %d",
      &p.last1, &p.last5, &p.last15,
      &p.active, &p.total, &p.lastPid);
    next = (next + 1) % loadData.length;
    sleep(500.msecs);
  }
```

[128]

Chapter 7

```
    }

    void index(HTTPServerRequest req, HTTPServerResponse res)
    {
      auto data = serializeToJson(loadData).toString;
      render!("index.dt", next, data)(res);
    }

    shared static this()
    {
      auto router = new URLRouter;
      router.get("/", &index);

      auto settings = new HTTPServerSettings;
      settings.port = 8080;
      settings.bindAddresses = ["::1", "127.0.0.1"];
      listenHTTP(settings, router);

      runTask(toDelegate(&collectLoadavg));

      logInfo("Please open http://127.0.0.1:8080/ in your
        browser.");
    }
```

3. The `index.dt` template file in the `views` folder uses JavaScript and the `canvas` element from HTML 5 to paint the graph:

```
doctype html
html
  head
    title Load average
  body
    canvas#graph(width="1200",height="200")
    script(type='text/javascript').
      var canvas = document.getElementById('graph');
      var context = canvas.getContext('2d');
      var next = #{ next };
      var data = #{ data };
      context.beginPath();
      context.moveTo(0, canvas.height);
      for (var i = next; i < data.length; i++)
        context.lineTo(i, canvas.height -
          1*data[i].last1*10);
      for (var i = 0; i < next; i++)
        context.lineTo(i, canvas.height -
          1*data[i].last1*10);
      context.stroke();
```

The vibe.d Internals

This example takes advantage of the fact that there is no synchronization required if fibers are used. The data in the `loadData[]` array is written by the `collectLoadavg()` function and read in the `index()` function. As a consequence, you cannot distribute the fibers across threads.

Using a thread

A thread is the right choice if your background task requires a lot of computations. A task with a long computation usually has no calls to pseudo-blocking functions. Using fibers, you would have to sprinkle calls to `yield()` over the function. A thread is better suited.

To simulate a long-running computation, you can compute a **Mandelbrot set**.

> If you've never heard of Mandelbrot sets, then you should read the Wikipedia article at https://en.wikipedia.org/wiki/Mandelbrot_set.

To simplify the coding, the picture is created as ASCII art. It looks as follows:

The computation is done in a separate thread. The fiber handling the request has to wait for the result of the computation. The implementation uses a so-called **future**. A future is a value that will be available in the future. It is represented with `struct Future`. The value is retrieved with the `getResult()` method. This methods blocks until the value is available.

> Synchronization between fibers and threads is not implemented in vibe.d 0.7.23.

The `async()` function is used to start the computation. It returns a `struct Future` instance. You can perform background work using a thread as follows:

1. Create a new project with dub:

   ```
   $ dub init mandelbrot --type=vibe.d
   ```

2. Change the `app.d` module in the `source` folder to contain the code computing the Mandelbrot set as an ASCII image:

   ```
   import vibe.d;

   // Maximum number of iterations
   enum MAX_ITERATION = 262144;
   // Maximum absolute value
   enum MAX_LENGTH = 100;
   // Set's boundary in the complex plane
   enum X_MIN = -2.1;
   enum Y_MIN = -1.1;
   enum X_MAX = 0.7;
   enum Y_MAX = 1.1;
   // Number of lines to compute
   enum RESOLUTION = 24;

   enum COLORS = " -:=+oxOX@#";
   enum xres = cast(int)(RESOLUTION*3.2);
   enum yres = RESOLUTION;
   enum xmin = X_MIN, ymin = Y_MIN;
   enum xstep = (X_MAX - X_MIN) / (RESOLUTION*3.2);
   enum ystep = (Y_MAX - Y_MIN) / RESOLUTION;

   char[][] mandelbrot()
   {
     char[][] pixels = new char[][](yres, xres);

     foreach (y; 0..yres)
   ```

```
      foreach (x; 0..xres)
      {
        // Calculate sequence for one value
        int iteration = 0;
        float z1 = 0.0, z2 = 0.0, t1 = void;
        do {
          t1 = z1*z1 - z2*z2 + (xmin + x*xstep);
          z2 = 2 * z1*z2 + (ymin + y*ystep);
          z1 = t1;
          iteration++;
        } while (iteration < MAX_ITERATION
          && z1*z1 + z2*z2 < MAX_LENGTH);
        int cindx = 0;
        do
          cindx++;
        while ((1 << cindx) < iteration);
        auto color = iteration >= MAX_ITERATION
          ? 0 : (cindx%COLORS.length);
        pixels[y][x] = COLORS[color];
      }

    return pixels;
  }

  void index(HTTPServerRequest req, HTTPServerResponse res)
  {
    auto pixels = async(&mandelbrot);
    auto result = pixels.getResult().join("\n");
    render!("index.dt", result)(res);
  }

  shared static this()
  {
    auto settings = new HTTPServerSettings;
    settings.port = 8080;
    settings.bindAddresses = ["::1", "127.0.0.1"];
    listenHTTP(settings, &index);

    logInfo("Please open http://127.0.0.1:8080/ in your
      browser.");
  }
```

3. The `index.dt` template file in the `views` folder only outputs the image:

   ```
   doctype html
   html
     head
     title Mandelbrot
     body
     pre #{result}
   ```

Using high-level synchronization constructs such as futures makes our life easier. The vibe.d framework supports standard synchronization methods such as **mutexes** and **condition variables** as well. Currently, it is important to use the versions from vibe.d and not the ones from the standard library. This restriction may change in the future versions.

Porting an existing driver

The vibe.d framework provides you with a rich set of database drivers and other I/O functionality. However, if you need access to another database, then you have to check whether the database driver supports vibe.d. The reason is the fiber-based pseudo-blocking model. A usual way to connect to a database is via TCP/IP. A standard C or D library creates a socket and uses this socket for communication. However, the standard functions block the calling thread. Using such a driver would stall your application: once the thread is blocked, every fiber is blocked as well. The solution is to replace all the blocking calls with an equivalent pseudo-blocking function.

Here are some guidelines:

- The socket class for stream-oriented communication is `TCPConnection`. This class replaces the `Socket` class from the standard library. An instance of this class is returned when you create a connection with `connectTCP()`. Most likely, you have to change the connection sequence completely. After the `TCPConnection` instance is available, it is used to send and receive data with the `read()` and `write()` methods.

- To send and receive UDP packets, you use the `UDPConnection` class. The `listenUDP()` function is the only function that creates an instance of this class. If you want to send UDP packets, you can use `0` for the port number.

- The functions and classes from the `std.stdio`, `std.file`, and `std.stream` files also block the calling thread and must be replaced. The vibe.d framework provides a rich set of file-oriented functions. The `readFile()`, `readFileUTF8()`, `writeFile()`, `appendFile()`, `copyFile()`, `moveFile()`, and `removeFile()` convenience functions handle files as a unit, for example, reading a file at once. The `openFile()` function returns a stream object that is suitable for random access. If you need a temporary file, then use the `createTempFile()` function.

- The functions to iterate a directory and retrieve file information must be replaced as well. The `listDirectory()` function calls a delegate for each file in a directory, `iterateDirectory()` returns a delegate usable with a foreach loop, `existsFile()` checks whether a file exists, and `getFileInfo()` returns the file information.

- If you need to check whether the files in a directory change, then you should use `watchDirectory()`. This functionality is not available in the standard library and can be simulated in the code.

- Do not use the synchronization constructs from `core.sync` together with fibers because these functions block the calling thread. The vibe.d framework provides the `TaskMutex` and `TaskCondition` classes as replacements. To exchange data between two tasks with the pipe pattern, use the `TaskPipe` class.

- Some restrictions also apply to the thread functions in `core.thread`, `std.parallelism`, and `std.concurrency`. Most notably, vibe.d provides its own version of `sleep()`. The message passing functions in the `std.concurrency` package currently block the thread as well. You can use the replacement functions from `vibe.core.concurrency`.

- Last but not least, there is a `Timer` class that is used to create timeout events.

You do not have to remember this list. If you are porting a driver, then ask yourself which function may block. All the I/O and thread-related functions are suspicious. Be aware that sometimes these functions are used under the hood. For example, memory allocation functions may use thread-related functions in order to provide thread-safe memory allocation. If you identify such a function, then search the vibe.d API documentation at `http://vibed.org/api/` for a replacement function. You can use the MySQL driver as a blueprint because this driver works with vibe.d and the standard library. You can find the source on GitHub at `https://github.com/mysql-d/mysql-native`. There is also a blog post that describes the needed steps in detail: `http://vibed.org/blog/posts/writing-native-db-drivers`.

An alternative solution for the existing drivers

It is not always possible to modify the source of an existing driver. The common problem is a closed source driver. In this case, you can link only against a library but you do not have the source.

The solution is to move the access to this driver to a separate thread or process. You must then create a communication channel between your application and this separate thread or process using the functions provided by vibe.d. The advantage of this solution is that you do not have to modify the source. The disadvantage is clearly the complexity introduced by the communication between threads and processes.

Summary

In this chapter, you learned about the fiber-based pseudo-blocking programming model of vibe.d. The building blocks of this model are asynchronous I/Os and fibers. They are used in such a way that the developer is shielded from the complexity most of the time. We are now aware that functions that block the calling thread must be replaced by equivalent functions provided by vibe.d in order to prevent the stalling of our application.

This programming model is very powerful and can be used in unusual ways, too. As an example, the next chapter shows how to use vibe.d with a GUI application.

8
Using vibe.d with a GUI Client

The fiber-based pseudo-blocking programming model that was introduced in the previous chapter is not restricted to web applications. An application with a **Graphical User Interface (GUI)** already uses an event loop, which can be easily integrated with vibe.d. You can then benefit from using fibers and avoid the complexity of threads.

In this chapter, we will cover the following topics:

- How to use a GUI event loop with vibe.d
- How to create a GUI application for Windows and X11 with vibe.d
- How to use other GUI toolkits

The GUI event loop and vibe.d

Every modern graphical user interface is event-based. The typical events are keystrokes, mouse moves, and requests to repaint a part of the screen. A common requirement is that you have to react quickly to the event. If you fail to do so, then your user interface seems to be frozen. Most of the time, it is recommended that you move long-running computations to a separate thread. While this sounds like a good idea, there are some pitfalls. Some systems allow only the thread running the event loop to draw on the screen. In this case, you have to synchronize with the event thread, which can get complicated very fast.

Using vibe.d with a GUI Client

Now, recall the fiber-based pseudo-blocking programming model from vibe.d, described in the previous chapter. An event queue is used to handle notifications that stem from asynchronous I/O. The processing is done in a fiber, which should quickly invoke the event loop again. As both concepts are so similar, the obvious idea is to combine both.

Depending on the user interface, vibe.d offers two different ways. On Win32, there is a native event driver implementation based on `MsgWaitForMultipleObjectsEx()` that allows the handling of Windows and I/O events together. If you are using X11, then you can retrieve the file descriptor for the display and use `createFileDescriptorEvent()` to create a new event to handle the X11 events.

Creating a Win32 GUI application

Due to the Win32 API, a Windows GUI application looks different from the other example applications in this book. If you are new to this topic and want to know more about it, then you should read *Programming Windows, Fifth Edition*, by *Charles Petzold, Microsoft Press*. You can find the book at http://www.informit.com/store/programming-windows-9780735692633.

The example application utilizes two fibers to draw rectangles and ellipses in two parts of the window screen. Due to the fiber-based approach, this is easy. The alternative is to use a timer event or separate threads, but this requires more coding. The Windows GUI application that you will create now looks as follows:

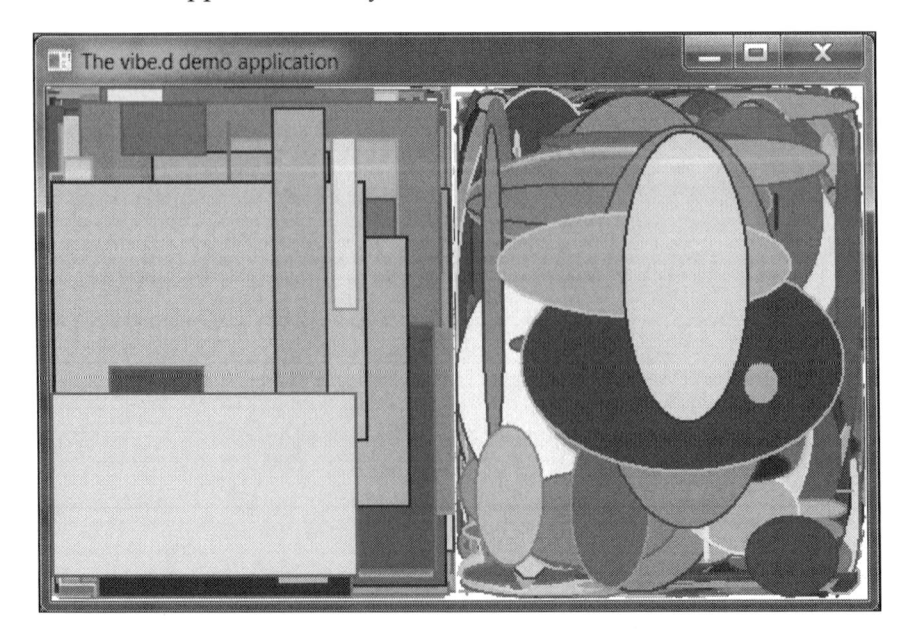

There is no special template for Win32 applications in `dub`. You can create a minimal project as follows:

```
$ dub init winclient --type=minimal
```

The generated `dub.sdl` file must be changed. The default `main()` function cannot be used—you have to specify the `VibeCustomMain` version. This is true for command-line parsing. You disable the parsing with the `VibeDisableCommandLineParsing` version. The vibe.d framework uses a different event handling implementation for Win32 applications. You have to explicitly choose the vibe.d configuration that you want to use. This is done with the `subConfiguration` keyword. The configuration is named `win32`. As the application must be linked with the `-Subsystem:Windows` option (the `lflags` keyword) and also requires the `gdi32.lib` library (the `libs` keyword), we create a configuration for our application as well. The `dub.sdl` file looks as follows:

```
name "winclient"
description "A Win32 GUI client using vibe.d."
copyright "Copyright © 2015, PACKT Publishing"
authors "Kai Nacke"
dependency "vibe-d" version="~>0.7.23"
versions "VibeCustomMain"
versions "VibeDisableCommandLineParsing"

configuration "win32" {
  platforms "windows"
  targetType "executable"
  libs "gdi32"
  lflags "-Subsystem:Windows"
  subConfigurations "vibe-d" "win32"
}
```

The `win32` configuration is the default, and only, configuration. If you are creating a cross-platform application, then you can add configurations for each supported platform.

There is only one source file, `app.d`, in the `source` folder. It starts by importing the required modules:

```
import vibe.core.core;
import core.runtime;
import core.sys.windows.windows;
import std.datetime;
import std.exception;
import std.functional;
import std.random;
import std.utf;
```

Using vibe.d with a GUI Client

The `vibe.core.core` module provides the event loop and task functions. The other stuff from vibe.d is not used. The `core.runtime` module is required because the D environment must be initialized manually. Finally, `core.sys.windows.windows` provides the Win32 API.

A confusing fact about the Win32 API is that every function that works with character data is available in two variants. One variant uses ANSI strings and the other uses UTF-16 strings. A suffix distinguishes the versions: the A suffix (as in `MessageBoxA`) denotes the ANSI variant and the W suffix (as in `MessageBoxW`) denotes the UTF-16 (wide character) variant. Internally, the ANSI-based functions recode the strings to UTF-16 and then call the UTF-16-based functions. It is, therefore, better to use the UTF-16-based functions. This goes nicely with D: the `wstring` type uses UTF-16 as well.

The code in the `main()` function is mostly the usual code required for a Win32 GUI application. First, the window class is registered and then a window based on this class is created. Finally, the window is shown. Some vibe.d specific code follows. Two fibers are created: one paints the rectangles and the other paints the ellipses. Instead of the usual Windows event loop, the `runEventLoop()` function is called:

```
int main(){
  wstring caption = "The vibe.d demo application";
  wstring className = "VibedWndClass";
  HINSTANCE hInstance = GetModuleHandleA(null);
  HWND hWnd;
  WNDCLASSW wndclass;

  wndclass.style       = CS_HREDRAW | CS_VREDRAW;
  wndclass.lpfnWndProc    = &WindowProc;
  wndclass.cbClsExtra   = 0;
  wndclass.cbWndExtra   = 0;
  wndclass.hInstance    = hInstance;
  wndclass.hIcon        = LoadIconA(null, IDI_APPLICATION);
  wndclass.hCursor      = LoadCursorA(null, IDC_ARROW);
  wndclass.hbrBackground = cast(HBRUSH)
              GetStockObject(WHITE_BRUSH);
  wndclass.lpszMenuName  = null;
  wndclass.lpszClassName = className.ptr;

  if (!RegisterClassW(&wndclass))
  {
    MessageBoxW(null, "Couldn't register Window Class!"w.ptr,
      caption.toUTF16z, MB_ICONERROR);
```

```
      return 0;
   }

   hWnd = CreateWindowW(className.toUTF16z, caption.toUTF16z,
      WS_THICKFRAME| WS_MAXIMIZEBOX |
      WS_MINIMIZEBOX | WS_SYSMENU | WS_VISIBLE,
      CW_USEDEFAULT, CW_USEDEFAULT,
      600, 400, HWND_DESKTOP, null,
      hInstance, null);

   if (hWnd is null)
   {
      MessageBoxW(null, "Couldn't create window."w.ptr,
         caption.toUTF16z, MB_ICONERROR);
      return 0;
   }

   UpdateWindow(hWnd);

   runTask!HWND(toDelegate(&paintRectangles), hWnd);
   runTask!HWND(toDelegate(&paintEllipses), hWnd);

   return runEventLoop();
}
```

Each window has a special procedure that is called to process events. In this case, there is not much to do. In case of a `WM_PAINT` event, the background is filled with the background brush (color white). This event is sent every time the screen needs some repainting. In case of a `WM_DESTROY` event, the event loop is terminated with a call to `exitEventLoop()`. This is again vibe.d-specific. The function only sends a `WM_QUIT` message to the thread running the event loop. The `quit` variable is set to true to stop the fibers. Remember that no synchronization is required here.

Every message is sent to the default window procedure as well:

```
bool quit = false;

extern(Windows)
LRESULT WindowProc(HWND hWnd, UINT message, WPARAM wParam,
   LPARAM lParam) nothrow
{
   switch (message)
   {
```

```
      case WM_PAINT:
        PAINTSTRUCT ps;
        HDC   dc = BeginPaint(hWnd, &ps);
        EndPaint(hWnd, &ps);
        break;

      case WM_DESTROY:
        quit = true;
        collectException(exitEventLoop());
        break;

      default:
        break;
    }

    return DefWindowProcW(hWnd, message, wParam, lParam);
}
```

The two fibers painting on the screen share similar code. A random number generator creates all the screen coordinates and colors. Painting uses the device context that is requested by the window handle. A pen is used to draw the outline of the figure while a brush is used to fill the interior. All the objects are released after drawing, and then the pseudo-blocking `sleep()` function is called to transfer control to the other fiber:

```
void paintRectangles(HWND hWnd)
{
  doPaint(hWnd, &Rectangle, false);
}

void paintEllipses(HWND hWnd)
{
  doPaint(hWnd, &Ellipse, true);
}

void doPaint(HWND hWnd, PaintFunc paint, bool placeRight)
{
  auto rnd(int bound) { return uniform(0, bound); }
  while (!quit)
  {
    auto hdc = GetDC(hWnd);
    scope(exit) ReleaseDC(hWnd, hdc);
    RECT r;
```

```
            GetClientRect(hWnd, &r);
            auto width = (r.right - r.left) / 2;
            auto height = r.bottom - r.top;
            auto left = rnd(width);
            auto right = rnd(width);
            if (placeRight) { left += width; right += width; }
            auto top = rnd(height);
            auto bottom = rnd(height);
            auto cPen = RGB(rnd(256), rnd(256), rnd(256));
            auto cBrush = RGB(rnd(256), rnd(256), rnd(256));
            auto hPen = CreatePen(PS_SOLID, 2, cPen);
            scope(exit) DeleteObject(hPen);
            auto hBrush = CreateSolidBrush(cBrush);
            scope(exit) DeleteObject(hBrush);
            SelectObject(hdc, hPen);
            SelectObject(hdc, hBrush);
            paint(hdc, left, top, right, bottom);
            sleep(100.msecs);
        }
    }
```

In order to be complete, some definitions are still missing. The `core.sys.windows.windows` module does not contain prototypes for all the GDI functions. You have to declare the missing functions yourself. The `PaintFunc` function type is also missing. Here is the last piece of the module:

```
    extern (Windows) {
    nothrow:
    BOOL Rectangle(HDC, int, int, int, int);
    BOOL Ellipse(HDC, int, int, int, int);
    HBRUSH CreateSolidBrush(COLORREF);
    alias PaintFunc = BOOL function(HDC, int, int, int, int);
    }
```

Using vibe.d with a GUI Client

Creating an X11 GUI application

The X11 application draws rectangles and ellipses as well. The structure of the application is basically the same but the details vary. `xlib`, the implementation library of X11, is not multithread-safe. The use of fibers here is a big win. The X11 GUI application that you will create now looks as follows:

Coding for X11 requires the development libraries. Depending on your operating system, you have to install them as follows:

- On Ubuntu/Debian, you can install the required library with the following command:

    ```
    $ sudo apt-get install libx11-dev
    ```

- On Fedora, you can type the following:

    ```
    $ sudo yum install -y libX11-dev
    ```

With the development libraries installed, you can create your project with dub:

```
$ dub init x11client --type=minimal
```

As in the Windows application, the minimal project type is used.

First, you update the generated `dub.sdl` file. The application requires a special `main()` function. Therefore, the `VibeCustomMain` version must be specified. The parsing of the command-line options is disabled with the `VibeDisableCommandLineParsing` version. Besides vibe.d, the application depends on X11. The `dub.sdl` file looks as follows:

```
name "x11client"
description "A X11 GUI client using vibe.d."
copyright "Copyright © 2015, PACKT Publishing"
authors "Kai Nacke"
dependency "vibe-d" version="~>0.7.23"
dependency "x11" version="~>1.0.8"
versions "VibeCustomMain"
versions "VibeDisableCommandLineParsing"
```

There is only one source file, `app.d`, in the `source` folder. It starts by importing the required modules:

```
import vibe.core.core;
import x11.X;
import x11.Xlib;
import std.datetime;
import std.functional;
import std.random;
import std.stdio;
import std.utf;
```

Instead of the Windows module, now two X11 modules are imported. An X11 application uses the standard `main()` function.

The first step is to open a display. This connects the client to the X server. The default screen is retrieved and a window is created. Before the window is made visible with `XMapWindow()`, the events that the application receives are limited to key press events. This is the basic code for an X11 application. In order to run the vibe.d event loop, an event is created from the file descriptor of the X11 connection, and the handling of X11 events is delegated to the `handleX11Events()` task. The two tasks to paint the graphic figures are created as well. After the event loop exits, the connection to the display is closed as follows:

```
int main()
{
  auto d = XOpenDisplay(null);
  if (d == null) {
    writefln("Cannot open display");
    return 1;
  }
```

Using vibe.d with a GUI Client

```
    scope(exit) XCloseDisplay(d);

    auto s = DefaultScreen(d);
    auto w = XCreateSimpleWindow(d, RootWindow(d, s),
        10, 10, 100, 100, 1,
        BlackPixel(d, s),
        WhitePixel(d, s));
    XSelectInput(d, w, KeyPressMask);
    XMapWindow(d, w);

    auto evt = createFileDescriptorEvent(ConnectionNumber(d),
        FileDescriptorEvent.Trigger.any);

    runTask(toDelegate(&handleX11Events), evt, d, s, w);

    runTask(toDelegate(&paintRectangles), d, s, w);
    runTask(toDelegate(&paintEllipses), d, s, w);

    return runEventLoop(); }
```

The X11 event handler task only has to deal with ending the application. The white background is automatically drawn if the window size changes. The `wait()` method of the event instance is used to wait for new events. If there is no event to handle, then this functions implicitly yields to another fiber. The handler reacts on two events: first, the window manager sends a message to close the window, and second, the user presses the *Q* key on the keyboard. As X11 has no concept of a window manager, there is no dedicated `CloseWindow` message. Instead, the window manager sends a `ClientMessage` message with a special payload. The *Q* key must be translated into the corresponding key code. If the handler detects that the application should exit, then the `quit` Boolean flag is set to true. No synchronization is required because fibers are used. Before the task ends, the `exitEventLoop()` function is called to stop the event processing:

```
    bool quit = false;

    void handleX11Events(FileDescriptorEvent evt, Display* d, int s,
        Window w)
    {
        Atom wmDeleteMessage = XInternAtom(d, "WM_DELETE_WINDOW",
            false);
        XSetWMProtocols(d, w, &wmDeleteMessage, 1);

        char[2] keySym = [ 'q', 0 ];
```

```
    immutable keyQ = XKeysymToKeycode(d,
      XStringToKeysym(keySym.ptr));

    XEvent e;

    while (!quit)
    {
      evt.wait();
      while (XPending(d))
      {
        XNextEvent(d, &e);
        if (e.type == ClientMessage &&
          e.xclient.data.l[0] == wmDeleteMessage)
          quit = true;
        if (e.type == KeyPress &&
          e.xkey.keycode == keyQ)
          quit = true;
      }
    }
    exitEventLoop();
}
```

The two fibers painting on the screen are similar to the fibers in the Windows application. The only functional difference is that no border is drawn around the figures. Both fibers again share similar code and call a provided function to paint on the screen:

```
void paintRectangles(Display* d, int s, Window w)
{
  doPaint(d, s, w, &XFillRectangle, false);
}

void paintEllipses(Display* d, int s, Window w)
{
  extern(C) int Ellipse(Display* disp, Drawable d, GC gc,
    int x, int y, uint width, uint height)
  {
    return XFillArc(disp, d, gc, x, y,
      width, height, 0, 360*64);
  }

  doPaint(d, s, w, &Ellipse, true);
}

void doPaint(Display* d, int s, Window w,
  PaintFunc paint, bool placeRight)
```

Using vibe.d with a GUI Client

```d
{
  auto rnd(int bound) { return uniform(0, bound); }
  while (!quit)
  {
    auto gc = XCreateGC(d, w, 0, null);

    static struct Geo {
      int x, y;
      uint width, height;
      uint borderwidth, depth;
    }
    Geo geo;
    Window root;
    XGetGeometry(d, w, &root, &geo.x, &geo.y,
      &geo.width, &geo.height,
      &geo.borderwidth, &geo.depth);
    auto halfwidth = geo.width / 2;
    auto x = rndhalfwidth);
    auto y = rnd(geo.height);
    auto width = rnd(halfwidth - x);
    auto height = rnd(geo.height - y);
    if (placeRight) x += halfwidth;

    auto cmap = XDefaultColormap(d, 0);
    XColor xcolor;
    xcolor.red = cast(ushort)rnd(xcolor.red.max);
    xcolor.green = cast(ushort)rnd(xcolor.green.max);
    xcolor.blue = cast(ushort)rnd(xcolor.blue.max);
    xcolor.flags = DoRed | DoGreen | DoBlue;
    XAllocColor(d, cmap, &xcolor);
    XSetForeground(d, gc, xcolor.pixel);

    paint(d, w, gc, x, y, width, height);
    XFreeGC(d, gc);
    sleep(100.msecs);
  }
}

alias PaintFunc = extern(C) int function(Display*, Drawable, GC,
  int, int, uint, uint);
```

There is one caveat: X11 is a network-based protocol. Some, but not all, X11 functions cause a network round-trip. For example, the `XGetGeometry()` function requires a network round-trip because the values have to be returned to the waiting client. Strictly speaking, these functions must not be called or a wrapper must be provided, which yields the processing of the other events. In this simple case, it does no harm, but you should not use such functions if you build an administration UI for a high-performance web server. In this case, you can handle `ConfigureEvent` and avoid the use of `XGetGeometry()`.

Integrating with other GUI toolkits

There are numerous other GUI toolkits available. The prominent examples are **GTK+** and **KDE**. The new Wayland server is intended as a replacement for the X server. The approach to integrate these toolkits is always the same: you need to find a way to process the GUI toolkit events with the vibe.d event manager. As vibe.d utilizes the widely used `libevent` library, you may get lucky and somebody may have already provided a solution. Alternatively, you can look for a `libev` solution. To use `libev` with vibe.d, you need to specify the `libev` configuration in your `dub.sdl` file:

```
subConfigurations    "vibe-d" "libev"
```

In case you have to roll your own implementation, you should take a look at `libasync`. This event loop library is written in D and the source is available on GitHub at `https://github.com/etcimon/libasync`. You can clone this repository and use it as a base for your integration task.

> Don't forget to create a pull request with your solution in order to make it available for others!

Summary

In this chapter, you learned how to use the fiber-based model from vibe.d with GUI toolkits. We also created a sample application for Windows and X11. Along with the previous chapters, we now have the knowledge to integrate other toolkits and extend the functionality of vibe.d.

The universality of vibe.d inspires a lot of extensions. The next chapter introduces some of the extensions created by the community.

9
Power Your Application with vibe.d Extensions

The vibe.d is a framework that can be extended easily. The D community has already created a lot of projects that use vibe.d and add new functionality. The ease of use is based on the DUB registry, which you can use for your projects as well.

In this chapter, you will learn the following topics:

- How you can publish your project and make it reusable by other developers
- Where to look for existing projects
- How to use some vibe.d extensions

Publishing your project in the DUB registry

The DUB tool automatically downloads the dependencies of your project. This is possible because there is a database with the available projects: the DUB registry. If you have created an open source project, then you should register your project in the DUB registry. The prerequisite is that you should use GitHub (https://github.com/), Bitbucket (https://bitbucket.org/), or GitLab (https://gitlab.com/) as your public code repository. You also need to check your `dub.json` file. The DUB tool generates a minimal version of this file containing default or generic values. To publish your project in the DUB registry, the `name`, `description`, and `license` fields are required. It is highly recommended that you assign meaningful text to the `authors` and `copyright` fields as well. After this preparation, you are ready to publish your project.

You can do so by going through the following steps:

1. Go to http://code.dlang.org/. If you do not have an account yet, then click on **Register** to register your user account. Otherwise, use the **Log in** menu to log in.
2. Click on the **My packages** menu. You can see a list of your already registered projects.
3. Click on **Register new package**.
4. Choose your repository provider and enter the name of the repository owner and the name of the repository itself. Then click on **Register package**.

Your project should be visible in the project listing at http://code.dlang.org/ in the next hour. The registry scans your project for changes about twice an hour. The changes are reflected to the project listing. To create a new version, you tag your code with a version label of the form, v1.2.3.

After you publish your project, other developers may want to include or reuse your code. However, is your code reusable? Here are some general guidelines that you should follow:

- If your project contains a main() function and produces an executable, then it is difficult for others to reuse some of your code. You can consider creating a library from part of your source. This requires a subPackages field in the dub.json file. Other projects can then depend on this subpackage.
- Provide usage examples if you are publishing a library. A good example can serve as the base to explore things. The vibe.d framework itself shows how to do this: create an examples folder and put all of your examples in this folder. In the dub.sdl file, you specify a dependency on the library using path. If your library is named examplelib, then the dub.sdl file looks as follows:

  dependency "examplelib" version="~master" path="../../"

- Think about customizations that others may need. Do not hardcode the configuration data but provide a Settings object instead, which others can use.

A brief summary of this is that code reuse must be planned. The reward is that more developers are likely to use your project.

Useful community projects

The DUB registry at `http://code.dlang.org/` is also useful if you are looking for some functionality. The following sections present some great projects from other developers, which you can integrate in your application.

Adding WebDAV services

WebDAV is an extension to the HTTP protocol. The acronym stands for **Web Distributed Authoring and Versioning**. With WebDAV, it is possible to create, move, and delete files and directories. To prevent parallel updates, a resource can be locked. In essence, WebDAV is a remote filesystem using HTTP as the transport protocol. There are client applications (including Windows Explorer) that can mount a filesystem exported with WebDAV. A well-known WebDAV server is the **Subversion** version control system; the latest version of a file can be retrieved with WebDAV.

There are several extensions built on top of WebDAV. One of them is **CalDAV**, the **Calendaring Extensions to WebDAV**. CalDAV uses WebDAV as the transport protocol and **iCalendar** as the data format to distribute scheduling information to clients. For example, **Lightning**, the calendar component of Mozilla Thunderbird, supports CalDAV calendars.

The `vibe-dav` project extends vibe.d with a WebDAV module and also adds basic support for CalDAV. An example including the setup of a calendar is distributed with the project. The interface is very simple. Here is how to serve some files:

1. Create a new project with `dub`:

   ```
   $ dub init davclient --type=vibe.d
   ```

2. Add a dependency to `vibe-dav` in the generated `dub.sdl` file:

   ```
   dependency "vibe-dav" version="~>0.4.6"
   ```

3. The `app.d` module in the `source` folder is changed in order to include the code to serve files from the `public` folder:

   ```
   import vibe.d;
   import vibedav.filedav;

   shared static this()
   {
     auto router = new URLRouter;
     router.serveFileDav("", "public");

     auto settings = new HTTPServerSettings;
     settings.port = 8080;
   ```

```
        settings.bindAddresses = ["::1", "127.0.0.1"];
        listenHTTP(settings, router);

        logInfo("Please open http://127.0.0.1:8080/ in your
          browser.");
    }
```

A platform-independent way to test the application is to use the **DAV Explorer**, which can be downloaded at `http://www.davexplorer.org/download.html`. The program is written in Java and requires a JVM to run. To launch the program, you type the following line on any Unix-like system:

```
$ DAVExplorer.sh
```

In Windows, you double-click on the `DAVExplorer.bat` file. Enter `http://127.0.0.1:8080/` as the URL and click on **Connect**. You should then see the files in the `public` folder.

Running your own blog

The vibe.d website features a blog at `http://vibed.org/blog/`. The application behind the blog is written in D and is available as the `vibelog` package. You can use the package as a standalone server or integrate it into your own application. MongoDB is used to store the articles.

Running the standalone application is very easy. After you have started MongoDB, you type the following to download and run `vibelog`:

```
$ dub fetch vibelog
$ dub run vibelog
```

The user interface of the standalone version is minimalistic but sufficient to learn the tool.

In order to post a blog entry, you have to go to the management page at `http://127.0.0.1:8080/manage/`. The page asks for a username that is `admin` with the password `admin` for the first login. For first-time configuration, you need to perform the following steps:

1. Click on **Manage Users** to create a new user. Activate the checkbox before the **admin** group to make the user an administrator.

2. Back in the menu, click on **Manage configurations**. You can see two entries: the active blog configuration (named **example** in the standalone version) and the **global** configuration.

   First, edit the global configuration. There is a textbox named **Categories**. This is the list of available categories for the blog. Each line represents a category. Enter at least one category and make sure that it contains no spaces. Then click on **Apply changes**. Edit the blog configuration. Check at least one of the listed categories for the blog. When you finish, click on **Apply changes**.

The blog is now configured. Click on **New post** to create your first blog entry! The created posts are shown on the index page at http://127.0.0.1:8080/.

The standalone version is nice because you can try the tool without any coding. For a real application, you want the blog shown in your website's theme and at least serve some static pages. In principle, the integration of the blog software is easy as well. The difficulty for a small demonstration is that the full UI is needed. For a quick start, you can copy the files from the standalone version in the following manner:

1. Create a new project with dub:

   ```
   $ dub init blog --type=vibe.d
   ```

2. Add a dependency to vibe-dav in the generated dub.sdl file:

   ```
   dependency "vibelog" version="~>0.4.2"
   ```

3. Copy the app.d module from the source folder in the vibelog folder to the source folder of the project. The module configures the necessary parts:

   ```
   import vibe.d;

   import vibelog.controller;
   import vibelog.web;
   import vibelog.webadmin;

   shared static this()
   {
     auto router = new URLRouter;

     auto blogsettings = new VibeLogSettings;
     blogsettings.configName = "my vibelog config";
     blogsettings.siteURL = URL("http://localhost:8080/");

     auto ctrl = new VibeLogController(blogsettings);
     router.registerVibeLogWeb(ctrl);
   ```

```
        router.registerVibeLogWebAdmin(ctrl);

        auto settings = new HTTPServerSettings;
        settings.port = 8080;
        listenHTTP(settings, router);
    }
```

4. Copy the templates from the `views` folder in the `vibelog` folder to the `views` folder of the project. Do the same with the `public` folder as well.

You have now copied the standalone version to a new project. The configuration is done in the `app.d` module and must be integrated with the configuration of your existing application. The following templates must exist:

- `vibelog.postlist.dt` is called if a list of postings should be shown
- `vibelog.post.dt` is called to show a single blog entry
- The `vibelog.admin.*.dt` templates contain the administration user interface

The controller for the views is provided in the `vibelog` package. The `vibelog.web.d` module contains the `VibeLogWeb` class that handles the requests and controls the views. Requests to the relative paths are described as follows:

- A GET request to /: This renders the list of postings using the `vibelog.postlist.dt` template. Optionally, a page number can be provided.
- A GET request to /posts/:postname: This renders the blog entry with `postname` using the `vibelog.post.dt` template.
- A POST request to /posts/:postname/comment: This adds a new comment to the `postname` blog entry.
- A GET request to /feed/rss: This returns an RSS feed.
- A GET request to /sitemap.xml: This returns a sitemap in an XML format.

You should be able to modify the UI as you like with this information.

Chatting with IRC

Connecting to an IRC server can be useful in several ways. You might want to implement a web interface for IRC or have some fun creating an **Eliza chat bot**. If you have never heard of Eliza, then you should visit http://nlp-addiction.com/eliza/ for the initial hands-on experience. Another application can be the posting of system events to a channel, for example, the successful running of unit tests.

The `vibeirc` module implements the IRC protocol and can be used for your application. The main class is named `IRCConnection`. You have to derive your own class from `IRCConnection` and override the following methods for the events that you are interested in:

Method	Called when...
`connected()`	This is called after the connection to the network is established. It returns `true` if the default login procedure is performed; otherwise, `false`.
`signed_on()`	This called after a successful login.
`disconnected()`	This is called after being disconnected.
`notice()`	This is called after the reception of an incoming notice.
`privmsg()`	This is called after the reception of an incoming private message.
`user_joined()`	This is called when a user joins the channel.
`user_left()`	This is called when a user leaves the channel.
`user_quit()`	This is called when a user disconnects from the network.
`user_kicked()`	This is called when a user is kicked out from the channel.
`user_renamed()`	This is called when a user changes the nickname.
`unknown_command()`	This is called when an unknown command is received.
`unknown_numeric()`	This is called when an unknown numeric command is received.

If you want to send a message, then you can use the `send_message()` method. The first parameter is the destination (channel or nickname) and the second parameter is the message. The optional third parameter specifies if the message is sent as a notice message. The default is to send the message as a private message.

Finally, the low-level method to send some data is `send_line()`. You can implement missing commands with this method, for example, `send_line("LEAVE #test")` to leave the `#test` channel.

A connection is established by calling `irc_connect()`. This method has your subclass of `IRCConnection` as a template parameter. An instance of the `ConnectionParameters` structure holds the details for the connection.

> Note that `username` defaults to `vibeIRC` if not specified.

The following is an implementation of a friendly bot. The bot joins the `#nice` channel and waits for your private messages. The message is logged and, depending on the receiver (nickname or channel), a different reply is sent:

1. Create a new project with `dub`:

    ```
    $ dub init irc --type=vibe.d
    ```

2. Add a dependency to `vibeirc` in the generated `dub.json` file:

    ```
    dependency "vibeirc" version="~>1.0.5"
    ```

3. The `app.d` module in the `source` folder is replaced with the following implementation of the bot:

    ```
    import vibe.d;
    import vibeirc;

    class Bot: IRCConnection
    {
      enum channel = "#nice";

      this()
      {
      nickname = "bot";
      }

      override void signed_on()
      {
      join_channel(channel);
      }

      override void privmsg(Message message)
      {
      if (message.isCTCP)
        return ;

      logInfo("[%s] <%s> %s", message.receiver,
                message.sender.nickname,
                message.message);
      if (message.receiver == nickname)
        send_message(message.sender.nickname,
              "Thanks for your message");
      else
    ```

```
        send_message(channel, "Thanks for using the channel");
    }
}

Bot bot;

static this()
{
    bot = irc_connect!Bot(ConnectionParameters("localhost",
                          6667));
}
```

Before starting this application, you must start an IRC server listening on port `6667` on `localhost`. The `vibeIRC` user must be able to connect without a password. The application connects to this IRC server and joins the `#nice` channel. If you send a message to the channel, then the bot replies with **Thanks for using the channel**. If you send the message to the bot, then the reply is **Thanks for your message**.

Coding for the Internet of Things

The vision of the Internet of Things is that intelligent devices communicate with each other to support the lives of human beings. An example is home automation. Sensors can measure the temperature in each room. This data is sent to an intelligent controller that regulates the heating or air conditioning based on this data. Other sensors record the open state of windows. You are then warned if you leave your home with the kitchen's window wide open. Or, even better, the window is closed automatically.

This kind of interaction between devices requires a lightweight protocol. MQTT is one such protocol. It is based on TCP/IP and designed for small network bandwidth. It uses a publisher-subscriber architecture, which requires a message broker to distribute messages.

A client connects to the broker in order to publish a message. A topic name belongs to each message. The topic name is the routing information for the broker. Each client that wants to receive messages subscribes to one or more topics. The broker uses the topic name to determine the clients to which the message is distributed. The topic name can consist of several hierarchies.

For example, a temperature sensor in the living room can publish the temperature with the `house/living-room/temperature` topic. A controller interested in the temperature of all the rooms can subscribe to the `house/+/temperature` topic. The + sign is the wild card for a single level; # can be used for multiple levels. Thus, a dashboard application that wants to monitor all the messages can subscribe to the `house/#` topic.

The `vibe-mqtt` library is a client library for the MQTT protocol. You can use this library to create your own publishers and subscribers. You still need a message broker. The possible choices are RabbitMQ (`https://www.rabbitmq.com/`), with the MQTT plugin enabled, or Mosquitto (`http://mosquitto.org/`). Be sure to use a recent version that supports MQTT 3.1.1.

Let's create an application with `vibe-mqtt`. For our examples, we use a publicly available MQTT broker provided by Mosquitto at `http://test.mosquitto.org/`. A publisher and subscriber share a lot of code. The central class is `MqttClient`. A publisher can instantiate an object of this class, connect to the broker, and start publishing messages. A subscriber is a bit more complicated. You have to create a subclass of `MqttClient` and override the following event methods that you are interested in:

Method	Called when...
onConnAck()	This is called when a connection acknowledge packet is received
onPingResp()	This is called when a response to a ping request is received
onPubAck()	This is called when a publish acknowledge packet is received
onPubRec()	This is called when a publish received packet is received
onPubRel()	This is called when a publish release packet is received
onPubComp()	This is called when a publish complete packet is received
onPublish()	This is called when a publish message packet is received
onSubAck()	This is called when a subscription acknowledge packet is received
onUnsubAck()	This is called when an unsubscription acknowledge packet is received

The packet types that are sent and received (and the method to be called) depend on the **Quality of Service** (**QoS**) used. The `vibe-mqtt` library fully supports level 0 (QoS0) with growing support for level 1 (QoS1) and 2 (QoS2). Using QoS0, you only need to override `onConnAck()` and `onPublish()` in order to subscribe to a topic.

An `MqttClient` instance is initialized with a `Settings` structure that holds the connection parameters. The most important one is `clientId`, which identifies the client and must be unique. If you play with multiple publishers or subscribers, be sure to use a different `clientId` for each one. Another important setting is `host`, which is the address of the broker.

The publishing application simulates a temperature sensor sitting in the living room. It sends the temperature in °C every two seconds. The subscriber application listens for all the messages and logs them with the information level. If you change `clientId`, then you can create publishing applications for other parts of the house as well:

1. Create a new project with `dub`:

   ```
   $ dub init mqttpublisher --type=vibe.d
   ```

2. Add a dependency to `vibe-mqtt` in the generated `dub.sdl` file:

   ```
   dependency "vibe-mqtt" version="~>0.1.1"
   ```

3. The `app.d` module in the `source` folder is replaced with the following implementation of the publishing application:

   ```
   import vibe.core.core;
   import mqttd;
   import std.random;
   import std.format;
   import core.time;

   shared static this()
   {
     auto settings = Settings();
     settings.host = " test.mosquitto.org ";
     settings.clientId = "living-room-publisher";

     auto mqtt = new MqttClient(settings);
     mqtt.connect();

     auto publisher = runTask(()
     {
       while (mqtt.connected)
       {
       float t = 20.0 + (10.0 - uniform(0, 20)) / 5.0;
       mqtt.publish("house/living-room/temperature",
             format("%0.2f", t));
       sleep(2.seconds);
       }
     });
   }
   ```

The publishing application runs in a loop but it does not output anything. You need a subscriber to the `house/#` topic to receive the messages:

1. Create a new project with `dub`:

   ```
   $ dub init mqttsubscriber --type=vibe.d
   ```

2. Add a dependency to `vibe-mqtt` in the generated `dub.sdl` file:

   ```
   dependency "vibe-mqtt" version="~>0.1.1"
   ```

3. The `app.d` module in the `source` folder is replaced with the following implementation of the subscriber application:

   ```
   import vibe.core.core;
   import vibe.core.log;
   import mqttd;
   import core.time;

   class Subscriber : MqttClient
   {
     this(Settings settings)
     {
     super(settings);
     }

     override void onPublish(Publish packet)
     {
     super.onPublish(packet);
     logInfo("Topic: %s Temperature in °C: %s",
         packet.topic, cast(string) packet.payload);
     }

     override void onConnAck(ConnAck packet)
     {
     super.onConnAck(packet);
     subscribe(["house/#"]);
     }
   }

   shared static this()
   {
     auto settings = Settings();
     settings.host = " test.mosquitto.org ";
     settings.clientId = "house-subscriber";

     auto mqtt = new Subscriber(settings);
     mqtt.connect();
   }
   ```

The subscriber application logs the received topic and temperature, so you can see what the publisher sends:

```
Topic: house/living-room/temperature Temperature in °C: 21.80
Topic: house/living-room/temperature Temperature in °C: 20.40
Topic: house/living-room/temperature Temperature in °C: 19.40
Topic: house/living-room/temperature Temperature in °C: 21.00
Topic: house/living-room/temperature Temperature in °C: 29.00
```

Serving news

A newsgroup is still an important communication channel. To distribute news, a news server is required. It is based on the NNTP protocol. To read the news, you connect a client, typically a mail program, to the news server. There are also web-based interfaces available. The `vibenews` package implements an NNTP server together with an HTTP client and administration interface. This package is different from the others presented here: you cannot customize it for your needs without changing the source. If you like the package, then you can use it either as a standalone application or as part of your application. The news articles are stored in MongoDB, so be sure to start the MongoDB server before you run `vibenews`.

The standalone application is downloaded and run with the following commands:

```
$ dub fetch vibenews
$ dub run vibenews
```

The Internet address and port number of the NNTP server and the administrator and client interfaces can be configured in the `settings.json` file. The administrator interface listens on port `9009` and the client interface on port `8009`. If you are using `127.0.0.1` as the Internet address, then you can use the URL, `http://127.0.0.1:9009`, to access the administrator interface. You can create newsgroups with the administrator interface and also manage users. If there is a problem with the database, then there is also an option to repair the newsgroup database. With the same setup, the client interface is available at `http://127.0.0.1:8009` and is a fully featured HTML client for the newsgroup. You should have a look at the D forum at `http://forum.dlang.org/` to get a feeling of how to use the application.

If you want to integrate `vibenews` into your application, then you need to add the following dependency to your `dub.sdl` file:

```
dependency "vibenews" version="~>0.6.6"
```

Additionally, you need to import the `app.d` module or copy this module to your application.

Accessing the Apache Cassandra database

Cassandra is a column-orientated NoSQL database from the Apache foundation. The website is `http://cassandra.apache.org/`. You can download the latest stable or development version from `http://cassandra.apache.org/download/`. The database is written in the Java language and requires a recent JDK to run. After downloading and unpacking the distribution file, you can start the database with the following command:

```
$ bin/cassandra -f
```

The `cassandra-d` project provides you with access to the Cassandra database. The API needs some polishing but you can use a lot of features. A simple client does not require too much code. The **Cassandra Query Language** (**CQL**) resembles SQL and is instantly usable if you are familiar with SQL. The application to access Cassandra database can be created as follows:

1. Create a new project with `dub`:

    ```
    $ dub init cassandra --type=vibe.d
    ```

2. Add a dependency to `cassandra-d` to the generated `dub.sdl` file:

    ```
    dependency "cassandra-d" version="~>0.0.3"
    ```

3. The `app.d` module in the `source` folder is replaced with the following implementation:

    ```
    import vibe.d;
    import cassandra.client;

    void main()
    {
        auto client = new CassandraClient("127.0.0.1");

        CassandraKeyspace keyspace;
        bool firstRun = false;
        try
        keyspace = client.getKeyspace("mykeyspace");
    ```

```
    catch (Exception e)
    {
      keyspace = client.createKeyspace("mykeyspace");
      firstRun = true;
    }

    struct User
    {
      int user_id;
      string fname;
      string lname;
    }

    if (firstRun)
    {
      keyspace.query("CREATE TABLE users "
              "(user_id int PRIMARY KEY, "
              "fname text, lname text)");
      auto table = keyspace.getTable("users");
      table.insert(User(1745, "john", "smith"));
      table.insert(User(1744, "john", "doe"));
      table.insert(User(1746, "john", "smith"));
    }

    auto result = keyspace.query("SELECT * FROM users");
    while (!result.empty)
    {
      User entry;
      result.readRow(entry);
      logInfo("%6s|%6s|%6s",
          entry.user_id, entry.fname, entry.lname);
    }
  }
```

The application connects to a running Cassandra database at localhost. Then, it tries to get `mykeyspace`. (A **keyspace** is similar to a schema in a relational database.) If this fails, the keyspace is created, and it is assumed that the application runs for the first time. If it is the first run, then a `users` table is created and three entries are inserted. The table is then queried for the data that it contains and the result is logged.

Summary

In this chapter, you learned how you can publish your project in the DUB registry and make it available for others. Developers from the D community have already done this and you used some of the projects that are already available. The wide range of the presented extensions should give you a lot of new ideas. With the knowledge that you gathered from this book, you can develop them quickly.

You are now well prepared to go beyond the topics of this book. The vibe.d framework is constantly developed and new features are added all the time. You can explore all the details that I haven't talked about. If you have created an application, then you should put it online and announce it to the D community. It is really rewarding to get positive feedback as I can tell you from my work on the LDC compiler.

Index

Symbol

@errorDisplay annotation
  error messages, displaying 75, 76

A

Apache Cassandra database
  accessing 164, 165
asynchronous I/O
  benefits 123, 124
  combining, with threads and fibers 124, 125
authentication
  adding 80-83

B

basic authentication
  about 54
  using 55-57
Binary JSON (BSON) 105
Bitbucket
  URL 151
blocks
  used, for integrating languages 23-27

C

CalDAV 153
Cassandra
  about 164
  URL 164
Cassandra Query Language (CQL) 164
certification authority (CA) 62
collection 88
community projects
  Apache Cassandra database, accessing 164, 165
  custom blog, executing 154-156
  Internet of Things, coding 159-163
  IRC, chatting with 156-159
  news, serving 163, 164
  WebDAV services, adding 153, 154
condition variables 133
CouchDB
  accessing 113
  API, URL 113
  installing 113
  NoteStore service, implementing 116-119
  REST interface, testing 113-116
  URL 113
Cross-site scripting (XSS)
  about 37
  URL 37
custom blog
  executing 154-156

D

D
  serializing, to JavaScript Object Notation (JSON) 104-106
data
  persisting, with MongoDB 94-96
database
  document database 87, 88
  key-value store 86, 87
  relational database 86
  selecting 85-88

DAV Explorer
  URL 154
D code
  adding, to templates 36, 37
D compiler
  building, from source 4-6
  DMD 2
  environment, verifying 6, 7
  GDC 2
  installing 2
  installing, on Debian 2, 3
  installing, on Fedora 3, 4
  installing, on OS X 4
  installing, on Ubuntu 2, 3
  installing, on Windows 4
  LDC 2
Debian
  D compiler, installing 2, 3
deimos project type
  about 7
  URL 7
D forum
  URL 163
Diet template
  creating 19
  HTML page, turning into 19-21
  includes, using 22, 23
  inheritance, adding 21, 22
  languages, integrating with blocks and filters 23, 24
Diet templates 12, 17
digest authentication
  about 54
  using 57, 58
DMD compiler
  reference link 6
  URL 2
document database
  about 87, 88
  advantage 88
  MongoDB, using 93
Don't Repeat Yourself (DRY) 19
D programming language
  about 1
  URL 1

driver
  porting 133, 134
  source, modifying 135
DUB package manager
  installing 2
  used, for setting up project structure 7-12
dub registry
  project, publishing 151, 152
  URL 152
dub.sdl file
  about 9
  fields 9
  reference link 9

E

Eliza chat bot
  URL 156
Erlang 113
error messages
  displaying, with @errorDisplay 75, 76
error page
  displaying 63-65
event methods
  onConnAck() 160
  onPingResp() 160
  onPubAck() 160
  onPubComp() 160
  onPublish() 160
  onPubRec() 160
  onPubRel() 160
  onSubAck() 160
  onUnsubAck() 160

F

Fedora
  D compiler, installing 3, 4
  URL 3
fiber-based pseudo-blocking programming model 121
fiber-based task
  executing 127-129
  performing 127

fibers
  about 121-123
  combining, with threads and asynchronous I/O 124, 125
files
  uploading 65, 66
filters
  css filter 24
  htmlescape filter 24
  javascript filter 24
  markdown filter 24
  used, for integrating languages 23-27
form-based authentication
  about 54
  TLS/SSL, enabling 62, 63
  using 59-61

G

GDC compiler
  URL 2
GitHub
  URL 151
GitLab
  URL 151
Graphical User Interface (GUI) 137
GTK+ 149
GUI event loop
  and vibe.d 137, 138
GUI toolkits
  integrating with 149

H

Homebrew package manager
  URL 4
HTML page
  turning, into Diet template 19-21
HTTP methods 69

I

iCalendar 153
includes
  using, for Diet template 22, 23

inheritance
  adding, to Diet template 21, 22
Internet of Things
  coding 159-163
IRC
  chatting with 156-159
IRCConnection class
  connected() method 157
  disconnected() method 157
  notice() method 157
  privmsg() method 157
  signed_on() method 157
  unknown_command() method 157
  unknown_numeric() method 157
  user_joined() method 157
  user_kicked() method 157
  user_left() method 157
  user_quit() method 157
  user_renamed() method 157

J

Jade templates
  URL 19
JavaScript Object Notation (JSON)
  about 87, 104
  D, serializing 104-106

K

KDE 149
keyspace 165
key-value store
  about 86, 87
  Redis, using 89
keywords, D
  URL 26

L

LDC compiler
  URL 2
libasync library
  URL 149

libcurl
  about 5
  URL 5
libevent
  URL 2
Lightning 153

M

main() function
  coding 125, 126
Mandelbrot set
  about 130
  URL 130
Markdown
  about 23, 24
  URL 24
MongoDB
  about 85
  data, persisting with 94-96
  installing 93
  URL 93
  used, as document database 93
Mosquitto
  URL 160
Multipurpose Internet Mail Extensions
      (MIME) 49
mutexes 133
MySQL
  installing 97
  URL 97
  used, as relational database 97
  using, with vibe.d 97-101
MySQL library 85

N

news
  serving 163, 164
note application
  about 39
  error page, displaying 63-65
  files, uploading 65, 66
  Redis, accessing 90-93
  session data, storing 50-54
  static files, serving 48-50
  template, creating 40-45
  user, authenticating 54, 55

note application, conversion
  about 69
  application, creating 71-74
  form field values, passing 70, 71
  handler functions, naming 69, 70
  sessions, creating 71
  session variables, creating 71
NoteStore service
  implementing 116-119
Null Object Pattern 52

O

object 104
OpenSSL
  URL 2
OS X
  D compiler, installing 4

P

Portable Operating System Interface
      (POSIX) 4
programming model, vibe.d
  about 121
  asynchronous I/O, benefits 123, 124
  fibers 121-123

Q

Quality of Service (QoS) 160

R

RabbitMQ
  URL 160
Redis
  about 85
  accessing, from note application 90-93
  installer, URL 89
  installing 89
  reference link 89
  URL 89
  used, as key-value store 89
relational database
  about 86
  advantage 86
  disadvantages 86

MySQL, using 97
Remote Procedure Call (RPC) 103
Representational State Transfer (REST) 103
REST API
  generated path, modifying 110-112
  parameters, passing 112
  tailoring 110
REST interface
  testing 113-116
REST service
  creating 107
  providing 107-109
  using 106-109
route matching 46, 47
routes
  associating, with handler functions 67-69
  initializing 67-69

S

Simple Declarative Language (SDLang)
  about 8
  URL 8
Simple Object Access Protocol (SOAP) 103
source tarball, DUB
  URL 3
SQL injection
  URL 37
static files
  serving 48-50
Structured Query Language (SQL) 86
Subversion version control system 153

T

templates
  basic syntax rules 20
  benefits 17-19
  comments, adding 29, 30
  common tasks, solving 28
  D code, adding 36, 37
  document type, configuring 28
  tags, adding 30
  website, localizing 31-36
threads
  combining, with fibers and asynchronous I/O 124, 125
  using 130-133

TLS/SSL
  enabling 62, 63

U

Ubuntu
  D compiler, installing 2, 3
Uniform Resource Locator (URL) 41, 104
user authentication
  basic authentication 54
  basic authentication, using 55-57
  digest authentication 54
  digest authentication, using 57, 58
  form-based authentication 54
  form-based authentication, using 59-62
  implementing 54, 55
user input
  error messages, displaying with @errorDisplay 75, 76
  validating 75
  validation, refining 77-80
user mode threads 123

V

vibe.d
  and GUI event loop 137, 138
  blog, URL 154
  MySQL, using 97-101
  programming model 121
vibe.d API
  URL 134
vibe.d framework
  about 1
  URL 1

W

web application
  creating 7
  project structure, setting up with DUB package manager 7-12
  template, creating 12-14
Web-based Distributed Authoring and Versioning (WebDAV) 153
web content
  localizing 83, 84

WebDAV services
  adding 153, 154
Web Service Description
        Language (WSDL) 103
Wget 127
Win32 GUI application
  creating 138-143
Windows
  D compiler, installing 4
World Wide Web (WWW)
  about 103
  principles, defining 104

X

X11 GUI application
  creating 144-149

Thank you for buying
D Web Development

About Packt Publishing

Packt, pronounced 'packed', published its first book, *Mastering phpMyAdmin for Effective MySQL Management*, in April 2004, and subsequently continued to specialize in publishing highly focused books on specific technologies and solutions.

Our books and publications share the experiences of your fellow IT professionals in adapting and customizing today's systems, applications, and frameworks. Our solution-based books give you the knowledge and power to customize the software and technologies you're using to get the job done. Packt books are more specific and less general than the IT books you have seen in the past. Our unique business model allows us to bring you more focused information, giving you more of what you need to know, and less of what you don't.

Packt is a modern yet unique publishing company that focuses on producing quality, cutting-edge books for communities of developers, administrators, and newbies alike. For more information, please visit our website at www.packtpub.com.

About Packt Open Source

In 2010, Packt launched two new brands, Packt Open Source and Packt Enterprise, in order to continue its focus on specialization. This book is part of the Packt Open Source brand, home to books published on software built around open source licenses, and offering information to anybody from advanced developers to budding web designers. The Open Source brand also runs Packt's Open Source Royalty Scheme, by which Packt gives a royalty to each open source project about whose software a book is sold.

Writing for Packt

We welcome all inquiries from people who are interested in authoring. Book proposals should be sent to author@packtpub.com. If your book idea is still at an early stage and you would like to discuss it first before writing a formal book proposal, then please contact us; one of our commissioning editors will get in touch with you.

We're not just looking for published authors; if you have strong technical skills but no writing experience, our experienced editors can help you develop a writing career, or simply get some additional reward for your expertise.

D Cookbook

ISBN: 978-1-78328-721-5   Paperback: 362 pages

Discover the advantages of programming in D with over 100 incredibly effective recipes

1. Leverage D to write efficient and correct programs with minimum code.
2. Learn advanced code generation techniques to automate programming tasks.
3. See how to apply D idioms to real-world problems and understand how it can benefit you.

Mastering D3.js

ISBN: 978-1-78328-627-0   Paperback: 352 pages

Bring your data to life by creating and deploying complex data visualizations with D3.js

1. Create custom charts as reusable components to be integrated with existing projects.
2. Design data-driven applications with several charts interacting between them.
3. Create an analytics dashboard to display real-time data using Node and D3 with real world examples.

Please check **www.PacktPub.com** for information on our titles

[PACKT] PUBLISHING open source
community experience distilled

Learning Web Development with Bootstrap and AngularJS

ISBN: 978-1-78328-755-0   Paperback: 224 pages

Build your own web app with Bootstrap and AngularJS, utilizing the latest web technologies

1. Build, develop, and customize your application using AngularJS and Bootstrap.
2. Utilize AngularStrap to pull in Bootstrap's jQuery plugins through Angular directives.
3. Packed with tips to help you avoid potential stumbling blocks while developing.

Learning Web Component Development

ISBN: 978-1-78439-364-9   Paperback: 256 pages

Discover the potential of web components using PolymerJS, Mozilla Brick, Bosonic, and ReactJS

1. Gain a practical understanding of web components through real-world examples.
2. Learn to construct a full and functional web component with native JavaScript.
3. Build your toolbox for web component development by harnessing the power of PolymerJS, ReactJS, Bosonic, and Mozilla Bricks.

Please check **www.PacktPub.com** for information on our titles

Printed in Great Britain
by Amazon